NEXT LEVEL LEADER

EUGENE WILSON

NEXT LEVEL LEADER

WORD AFLAME PRESS
WELDON SPRING, MO

Word Aflame Press
36 Research Park Court
Weldon Spring, MO 63304
pentecostalpublishing.com

Cover design by Jeremy Hart

Printed in the United States of America

Library of Congress Cataloging-in-Publication Data

Names: Wilson, Eugene, author.
Title: Next-level leader / by Eugene Wilson.
Description: Weldon Spring, MO : Word Aflame Press, [2024] | Summary: "Leadership development for pastors and church leaders"--Provided by publisher.
Identifiers: LCCN 2024019037 (print) | LCCN 2024019038 (ebook) | ISBN 9780757766008 (paperback) | ISBN 9780757766015 (epub)
Subjects: LCSH: Leadership--Religious aspects--Christianity.
Classification: LCC BV4597.53.L43 W573 2024 (print) | LCC BV4597.53.L43 (ebook) | DDC 253--dc23/eng/20240515
LC record available at https://lccn.loc.gov/2024019037
LC ebook record available at https://lccn.loc.gov/2024019038

CONTENTS

INTRODUCTION

Much like the scenario where a preacher delivers a sermon to himself, this book, to a certain degree, arises from a personal yearning for growth. I am writing to myself. I want to grow. In doing so, I am leaning heavily on self-reflection.

Looking back at my leadership journey, I see difficulties and struggles. But I also see growth. And the joy of growth far outweighs the pain. I imagine that my future will in many ways mirror my past. There will be times of difficulty and struggle. But, as in the past, the future will unveil joy in growth. To me that is remarkable.

Yes, sometimes growth hurts. Ultimately, however, our trials are vital to our being conformed to Christ. If not, what exactly would being conformed to Christ entail?

Indeed, being conformed to Christ is about aligning one's character and behavior to the teachings and values of Jesus Christ. It is taking upon oneself His character. It is about developing compassion and humility. It is about forgiving. It is about letting go of the desire to be vengeful.

It is about not allowing pain to cause one to become callous. It is about "counting it all joy."

Being conformed to Christ should be the ultimate pursuit of a next-level leader, not the fulfillment to lord it over others, and certainly not the making of one's own kingdom.

Regardless of where you might be in your journey—whether you are currently joyful in your trials or fighting against the very methods God is using to conform you to His nature—this book can assist you. It is challenging. Thought-provoking. Practical. Principle-driven. And, as stated, it is written from the mindset of someone who desires to grow.

You might ask, "What is a next-level leader?" A next-level leader, as portrayed in this book, is an individual who has taken on or is poised to take on an advanced tier of leadership. This progression often entails stepping into new roles and embracing additional responsibilities, signifying a need to move beyond one's current level of expertise and operation.

Achieving the next level of leadership typically demands the growth of skill sets and mindsets or the extension and improvement of existing ones. Hence, this book also addresses the importance of being stretchable, resilient, and adept at managing chaos. It underscores the value of deferring affirmation, embracing loneliness, and establishing a new rhythm. It delves into the importance of relinquishing the need for control, advocates active listening, exhorts its readers to be attentive to organizational culture, and more. All of which are crucial elements in achieving success at the next level.

I do not know everything God has in mind for my future. I can only imagine and listen to what He is speaking to me. I suspect the same is true for you. I do know this, however: the things God has in mind are bigger than what we can imagine. Hence, the need for growth.

Welcome to *Next-Level Leader*, a book crafted not just for those who lead but for those who aspire to do so at another level.

CHAPTER 1

BE STRETCHABLE

Many people know his story; thus, it would be easy to overlook its message. Like others, he harbored a dream of ascending to realms of higher leadership. He did not know how it would happen; the detailed steps were unclear. But the calling, the vision, the tug in his spirit—it was all genuine. He knew it—he was meant to go to the next level.

The young man, however, couldn't have fathomed the challenges he would encounter. Preparation for the next level would prove to be extensive. Pain, struggle, betrayal, being overlooked, and more were all a part of his story. Most interesting though, is that his journey and all that accompanied it equipped him for a great purpose—one bigger than he had imagined. He was destined to impact the world. His original dream would pale in comparison to what God had in mind. But isn't that just like God? His plans are always greater.

God's plans for you are greater too. Just like Joseph had to be prepared, you must be equipped for what God has in mind. It is doubtful, however, that you comprehend the extent to which you, like Joseph, will be stretched.

Preparation Is a Must

Throughout Scripture, we encounter instances where God called people and then began the process of preparing them. This preparation was crucial to enable them to fulfill the purpose for which they had been anointed. Thus, anointing and calling were not enough. Neither was giftedness. They had to be prepared to live out their calling.

Some years ago, while driving a van of young people to a youth convention, I asked a young person, "What do you want to do with your life?" With great excitement and wonderment, the young lady proceeded to tell me her plans for her future. I don't recall all the details, but I do remember thinking that her season of preparation would involve much more than she anticipated. So I said, "I believe in you." Then added, "But you will likely go through some stuff you are not expecting, and it might take some time before you step into the future you envision." I quickly added, "I don't say these things to discourage you; rather, to encourage you. When you encounter times of difficulty, don't stop. Don't quit. Stay with it, because God's hand is on your life."

As her future unfolded, much of what I said came to pass. After graduating from high school, she met a young man, and they married. I thought at the time, *He's not good for her.* But she was in love. Unfortunately, it wasn't long before her anticipated future with its timeline and details fell apart, and the couple divorced due to his infidelity and abuse. She entered a season of healing, and it was a difficult period for her as she faced many challenges.

In time, she remarried. A few years later, she launched a ministry to assist others who are walking a similar journey, and she is making a difference. While it isn't the future she once dreamed of, in many ways it is greater. It all depended, and still depends, on her openness to being stretched.

Stretched

Luke 2:52 states, "And Jesus increased in wisdom and stature, and in favour with God and man." As God, Jesus needed no growth. But as a man, He needed to be stretched. The picture depicted in Luke's writings is that His growth was well-rounded. Not only did Jesus increase in physical height, but He also grew in wisdom, meaning that He grew in His knowledge of both human and divine things.

According to *Thayer's Lexicon,* such growth is acquired by experience and acuteness, or an awareness of all things, including small things. Some, however, suggest that Jesus' development involved more than that. Regardless, the point is that He grew. Interestingly, following Luke's assertion that Jesus increased in wisdom and stature, there is nearly a two-decade silence regarding His life. It wasn't because nothing was happening. Jesus was still growing; He was being stretched. When His story picked back up, it was clear that He was prepared for His mission.

Stretched Defined

What is the essence of being stretched? The transitive form of the verb *stretch* denotes extension, while its intransitive counterpart signifies expansion without breaking. Consequently, to possess stretchability implies the capacity to expand without breaking, embodying a quality of adaptable resilience.

It is inherent in human nature to desire things to align perfectly to minimize the potential for chaos. We often assume that everything should unfold seamlessly, particularly when we believe we are divinely anointed. However, this perception is often distant from reality, as reality is frequently accompanied by difficult trials. Thus, when God has bestowed grand plans upon us, we should anticipate substantial resistance. The magnitude of the dream corresponds directly to the necessity for personal growth and expansion. In essence, the bigger the dream, the bigger the need to be stretched.

Advancing to the next level necessitates venturing into unfamiliar terrain and confronting experiences that may be entirely new. One cannot stay stagnant and expect to reach the next level; it doesn't unfold in that manner. Fluidity becomes paramount. Growth is not just beneficial; it is imperative. Change is not merely recommended; it is essential. To fulfill God's plans for our lives, we cannot remain as we are. We must actively embrace growth and willingly undergo the transformative process of being stretched.

If you find yourself being stretched, understand this: God is preparing you for something greater, something more substantial. Much like Joseph, you are undergoing a stretching.

Joseph's Greatest Test

Joseph's story is filled with heartache and triumph. He was placed in a pit, a literal low. He likely battled disappointment, discouragement, and maybe even depression. Of course we have no way of knowing this; we can only read between the lines and imagine ourselves in similar circumstances of betrayal, character assassination, and abandonment.

What exactly did God have in mind with Joseph being sold into slavery? What did He have in mind with Joseph's service in Potiphar's household? Why the temptation to succumb to the advances of Potiphar's wife? Why the lie, "He tried to rape me"? What was the purpose of the imprisonment? And why was Joseph forgotten by the butler?

Psalm 105:19 offers some insight. "Until the time that his word came: the word of the LORD tried him." The verse suggests that Joseph's greatest trial wasn't the pit or the prison. Nor was it any of the factors that led to his being cast into the pit or the prison. Joseph's greatest trial was the word of God. After having the dream, Joseph lived for years in circumstances that completely contradicted that dream. In his dream, his parents and brothers were to bow down to him; in reality, Joseph was the servant that had to bow down. What confused Joseph and tried his spirit was the precise word he had heard from God and the fact that his life was contrary to it. Think about it. He experienced twenty-plus years between the original dream and its fulfillment. Joseph was tried by the word of God for over two decades before the word of the Lord came to pass.

What was the purpose of Joseph's test? The answer is that God was preparing him for something greater than he had dreamed. What God had in mind was bigger than what Joseph had in mind. It was bigger than what God had revealed to him. God was setting Joseph up for something greater; He planned to use Joseph to save many people. Joseph's difficulties were designed for his development. He needed to grow; he needed to be stretched. He was nowhere near ready to assume the second most powerful position in the world, right next to Pharaoh. Yes, he had a dream. But a dream in and of itself wasn't enough. Joseph needed to be stretched to step into the next level of leadership. So God stretched him.

His first leadership position was within Potiphar's household, but it was only a short time before he outgrew his job. Thus, he needed to be stretched again. God had called Joseph to an enormous position, but he needed to be prepared for it. Hence, the prison. Joseph became the warden's favorite, and the warden put him in charge over all the other prisoners and over everything that happened in the prison. It was another step in the preparation process because God's plan was that Joseph would, in time, become the manager of Egypt. He eventually was made overseer of a vast amount of grain that delivered Egypt and many other people from a famine. But first, he had to be stretched.

Things to Consider While Being Stretched

If we are going to fulfill God's plan and purpose for our lives, we will experience times when we are stretched in order to grow. Consequently, there will be times when we are uncomfortable. There will be times when we are tempted to retreat. But growth doesn't come while hiding in the shadows; we must embrace the journey of growth if we are going to see our dreams come to fruition.

Cultivate a Growth-versus-Fixed Mindset

Numerous studies underscore the benefits of cultivating a growth mindset over a fixed mindset. One prominent example is a study led by psychologist Carol Dweck, in which the brain activity of children was analyzed following mistakes made on tests. The children entrenched in a fixed mindset displayed minimal activity during the review of errors, while their counterparts with a growth mindset demonstrated active cognitive processing.

Dweck, the originator of the terms *growth mindset* and *fixed mindset*, developed these concepts in her book *Mindset: The New Psychology of Success* (2006). According to Dweck, individuals operating from a fixed mindset perceive intelligence, abilities, and talents as static attributes rather than areas open to improvement. This distinction underscores the transformative potential of embracing a growth mindset, where capacities are viewed as dynamic and ripe for enhancement.

The implications of the different mindsets are vast. Someone with a growth mindset views challenges as opportunities for learning. While the challenge may be difficult to overcome, the outcome will be well worth the effort. On the other hand, a challenging situation can be catastrophic for someone with a fixed mindset. Such a person may think that without the required skills, talent, or intelligence, there is nothing that can be done, and there is no chance of improvement. Such thinking is limiting because it leads the person to act in limiting ways.

In contrast to the "there's nothing I can do about it" thought process, an individual with a growth mindset engages in behaviors that contribute to personal development, enabling one to effectively navigate challenges. Resilience emerges as the pivotal factor, playing a vital role in surmounting obstacles. Individuals with a fixed mindset frequently exhibit a shortage of resilience, whereas those embracing a growth mindset excel in it. Consequently, those with a growth mindset are best equipped to thrive in the midst of challenges.

Think Big Picture

I can vividly recall a period in my life marked by profound frustration. It occurred during a season of transition. I had several conversations involving potential financial support that could have propelled us forward. This would have helped cover moving costs, and it would have launched a nonprofit leadership initiative designed to impact thousands. I eagerly anticipated these opportunities, relying on what had been discussed and looking forward to a promising future. However, the anticipated support did not materialize.

During this challenging time, I learned a pivotal lesson: do not confine God to your expectations. Embrace thinking that goes beyond your limitations; envision a bigger picture. As I allowed my perspective to expand, my initial frustration transformed into excitement. I began to imagine possibilities beyond my initial considerations.

Today much of what I envisioned has become my reality, and more is yet to come. I'm grateful for the doors that didn't open as I once hoped. God meant for me to walk the path I have taken. I have learned that being stretchable requires thinking beyond one's current situation, mindset, and expectations.

Don't Stop Learning

A key factor to remaining stretchable is embracing learning. While returning to school may not work for you, it does for many. However, one does not have to attend college to learn. Consider the following:

- In today's world, technology offers multiple opportunities for growth. Masterclasses, YouTube videos, and TED Talks are just a few.

- Reading is also a great way to learn, primarily academic articles, many of which can be found online for free. Just google "free academic articles on _______." Fill in the blank with whatever is needed.
- If you don't enjoy reading, consider short summaries or audiobooks.
- Consider hiring a coach, even if it is just for a short period.

The bottom line is you have no excuses. There is great danger in plateauing, so don't stop learning.

God's Got Something More in Mind

God is up to something bigger than what we readily recognize. This is why there's a pressing need for us to undergo stretching experiences. Much like Joseph, we may only perceive a fraction of what God is orchestrating; the entirety remains beyond our comprehension. When God bestows dreams to us, calls us, anoints us, or imparts prophetic words to us, the vastness of His intentions goes beyond our grasp. There is always more, always a grander design than we can fathom.

The story of the healing of my dad's twin brother and what happened afterward is a great example of how God had something big in mind—something bigger than what we were thinking. My uncle fell off a porch at the age of five years old, and because of his fall, he suffered from seizures, at times as many as three or four per week. Things changed when a relative invited my grandparents to visit a Pentecostal church.

When the song leader stepped forth to lead the congregation in worship, my grandfather looked at my grandmother and said, "Noie, when we get out of here, we are not coming back." My grandfather did not like the song leader, as he used to fight him in the bars over my grandmother. While leaving the building, the song leader came up from behind my grandfather, wrapped his arms around him, and said, "Johnnie, I'm not the same man." On the way home, my granddaddy remarked to my grandmother, "Noie, if God can change Coyt, he can change anyone. We are going back."

My uncle went to the altar on a Sunday not long after. God filled him with the Holy Ghost, called him to preach, and healed him of his seizures. He has never had another one. But God had something else in mind. My dad and his older brother also became ministers, and their sister married a minister. Many of my cousins and siblings and several of our children have entered the ministry. My uncle needed a miracle, and he received one. But God had something more in mind.

Conclusion

God loves us too much to leave us as we are; God wants us to grow. While in prison, Joseph quickly rose to the position of a trusted manager. He didn't have freedom. He didn't have power over his own life. He didn't have much at all, but he did have a calling from God to manage others. So that is what he did; he became a faithful manager at a low point.

If Joseph's life teaches us anything, it teaches us that difficulties and hard times can be used by the Lord in preparing us for what He has in mind. Like Joseph, we can say God meant it for good despite the enemy's evil intentions. His plan and purpose for our lives will be fulfilled if we persevere through challenges. If you find yourself being stretched, understand this: God is preparing you for something greater, something more substantial. God has something more in mind.

CHAPTER 2

BE RESILIENT

Numerous examples in Scripture highlight God's capacity to act swiftly and instantaneously. However, it is equally evident that God sometimes operates at a deliberate and measured pace. One compelling illustration is found in the journey of the children of Israel. The direct route through the land of the Philistines was the quicker path, yet God opted to guide the people through the longer route, the wilderness of the Red Sea. (See Exodus 13:17–18.) God's deliberate choice of the slower route emphasizes that His timing and methods often transcend human expectations, and that the longer path may hold valuable lessons and purposes that we may overlook on the swifter routes.

Scripture reveals the reason why God led the people the long way around. He knew that if Israel proceeded on the Philistine Road, they would encounter fierce resistance from the Philistines. If that were to happen, the Israelites may have gone back to Egypt. It was going to take time for the people to become dependent on God, time for the people to become *His* people.

In chapter 14, the exodus story took an unexpected turn when the people became hemmed in by the desert and the Red Sea. Pharaoh, having observed the wanderings of the people and witnessing their predicament, was enticed to capture the former slaves and return them to Egypt. Of course, his plans were thwarted as God's purpose prevailed. God miraculously parted the waters, and the children of Israel crossed over on dry ground. Pharaoh's army pursued, but God released the held-back waters. Israel was saved, Pharaoh's army was destroyed, and God was glorified.

Yet the journey was far from over; in fact, it had just begun. Shortly after hearing an unfavorable report, the people rebelled against God and yearned for Egypt. In response, God directed them on an extended path that led to forty years of wandering. It might have seemed aimless to some, but it was purposeful—God's purpose. The extended journey served as a profound period of learning: learning to follow, learning to trust, learning resilience, and cultivating dependence on Him. The pillar of cloud by day and pillar of fire by night symbolized this purpose. When the pillar moved, the people followed; when it stopped, they stopped. Everywhere the pillar went, the people went. In following the cloud and fire, the people were learning to follow God.

What Is Resilience?

Resilience is the ability to withstand difficulties or to recover from them as quickly as possible. It is about being able to adjust to disruptive change and maintain one's energy level in the face of heightened pressure.

Maneuvering through challenges is part of leadership. Leading others is not easy. Those who follow will, from time-to-time, question their leader's purpose. The lack of certainty regarding the future will cause some individuals to strongly resist change. Leading others demands conviction, courage, and resilience.

Next-level leaders are resilient. In times of difficulty, they become stronger. They grow. When they encounter setbacks, they bounce back. They lead in healthy ways despite what they face.

Grit is closely associated with resilience. Whereas resilience is the ability to recover from or easily adjust to difficulties, grit is the courage and resolve to endure. It is about maintaining passion to continue moving forward despite difficulties. It is about perseverance.

Studies indicate that an individual's grit level is a strong predictor of success. Notably, one's level of grit more accurately predicts task completion across various domains than both talent and IQ.

Gritty leaders are in it for the long haul. They are focused. Setbacks do not deter them. Setbacks make them stronger and more determined to find a way.

Next-level leaders need both resilience (the ability to recover from setbacks) and grit (the courage to endure). Situations will arise that will challenge next-level leaders. The unexpected will happen. Hard times will come.

Resilience and grit are needed for a next-level leader not only to survive but thrive.

Moses

Moses was resilient. As a next-level leader, he certainly had his hands full. After four hundred years of bondage, the people had been impacted in multiple negative ways. Change, although greatly desired, was not going to be easy. It would require a new mindset, a new way of seeing things. For the first time, the people heard God speak, and it scared them. The giants scared them too, as did their imposing, fortified cities. It was all very new and very scary.

It wasn't easy for Moses to lead scared people. Individuals gripped by fear are frequently resistant to change. Moses had to embody resilience in the face of this daunting task. He had to adapt; he had to learn how to lead others through disruptive changes and do so in a healthy manner despite the resistance and difficulties.

It is evident that Moses also displayed grit. Although he experienced times of frustration, he stayed with it, enduring the ups and downs of his assignment. He endured forty years of wandering in a wilderness. Forty years of raising up a new generation, one that would trust God in moving forward to possess the Promised Land. Indeed, Moses was both resilient and gritty.

Likewise, we are called to be both resilient and gritty while leading others, especially during times of major upheaval and change. Such is the life of a next-level leader.

David

We do not know how old David was when he was anointed by the prophet Samuel. Neither do we know how old he was when he killed Goliath. Biblical scholars estimate he may have been between thirteen and seventeen years old. We do know, according to II Samuel 5:3–4, that David was thirty years old when he was anointed king over a portion of the kingdom. It was another seven years and six months before he was anointed a third time, this time over the entire kingdom. This means some twenty-plus years transpired from the time Samuel anointed David to the fulfillment of the anointing.

Let's consider the life of David between the anointings:

- After being anointed by Samuel, David returned to taking care of his father's sheep.
- David served as a musician in Saul's court.
- David killed Goliath.
- King Saul attempted to kill David.
- King Saul fired David from his court, then appointed him a captain in his army.
- Because of jealousy, Saul threatened David with bodily harm.
- David hid in the city of Gath and pretended to be a crazy man.
- David recruited an army.
- David lived in the wilderness.
- David was tempted to kill King Saul but refrained from doing so.

Here are a few lessons we can glean from David's life regarding being resilient:

- Embrace the role of a servant. After being anointed, David returned to taking care of the sheep.
- Rid yourself of the root of bitterness. David refused to allow bitterness to destroy his life.
- Do not become vengeful; that is for the Lord and the Lord alone. David refrained from taking matters into his own hands.
- Practice patience. David overcame the temptation to ascend to the throne before God's time.

No doubt many other lessons can be gleaned from David's resiliency. Perhaps the most important lesson we can derive from David's life between the anointings involves his grit. David persevered through challenging times; he did not give up. Despite the considerable time gap between his initial anointing and its eventual fulfillment, David remained steadfast and committed. He was gritty.

We also glean from David's example that it isn't the initial anointing alone that determines our future; it is the life we live after we are anointed that has a large bearing on our destiny. Being gritty matters.

Enduring the Long Haul

Jesus sounded a warning in Matthew 24 concerning the end time. Many who considered themselves to be followers would turn away from their faith. They would be offended. They would betray one another and hate one another. False prophets would arise and deceive many. Wickedness would increase, and the love of many would fade away.

One paraphrase of the passage reads as such:

> It will be dog-eat-dog, everyone at each other's throat, everyone hating each other. In the confusion, lying preachers will come forward and deceive a lot of people. For many others, the overwhelming spread of evil will do them in—nothing left of their love but a mound of ashes. Staying with it—that's what God requires. Stay with it to the end. (Matthew 24:9–14, *The Message* by Eugene Peterson)

We tend to think that "false prophets" are easy to spot and thus, easy to reject. But if that were true, then many would not be deceived by them. Yet many are.

False prophets tell us what we want to hear, not what we need to hear. We want to hear, "You are stepping into your destiny!" "Goodbye to hardship and trials! Hello to health, wealth, fame, and fortune!" We like such prophecies. We want to hear that our struggle is almost over.

The truth is quite different. I once heard of a theologian (I have long forgotten who it was) who said that giving your life to the Lord is more like "Come to Jesus and let Him mess up your life." In other words, living for Jesus isn't always rosy.

Every step taken is a step into one's destiny. But it is deeply discouraging to walk as the children of Israel did for forty years and not step into the Promised Land.

We want to believe it is going to happen now—and it could. But it is more likely that much time will transpire before we step in and possess all God has promised us. It is often an "already, not yet" phenomenon. It is done. Completed. God has given it to us, yet we must "live it" into existence. We must contend. We must endure.

As next-level leaders, we should embrace resilience and grit. We should live in an "already, not yet" state. This phenomenon isn't easy to navigate, but it is necessary nonetheless.

Developing Endurance

How does one develop endurance—the ability to be persistent? How does one gain grit?

James offered some insight when he wrote,

> Count it all joy, my brothers, when you meet trials of various kinds, for you know that the testing of your faith produces steadfastness. And let steadfastness

> have its full effect, that you may be perfect and complete, lacking in nothing. (James 1:2–4, ESV)

According to James, we develop grit by going through tough things that we don't enjoy—and yet we are to count it joy. How is that possible? It is possible when we understand that what we are going through—if we are resilient and gritty—will produce something wonderful.

Joseph's life serves as a wonderful example. He developed persistence and steadfastness while in the pit. He developed it while serving in Potiphar's household. He honed it while he was in prison. The ability to stay with something does not come in the good times; it comes in times of difficulty. Times of difficulty produce grit, but only if you stick with it.

Greater Things

"Good is the end of great," said author Jim Collins in the opening sentence of his book *Good to Great*. I vividly remember saying something similar long before Collins's book existed. My deep desire for what was best is why I said it: "I don't want to look in the mirror twenty years from now and think, *It has been good*. Instead, I want what is best." You should too.

The challenge, however, is that most often *what is best* comes about through difficulty. Hence, if you are experiencing struggles, know that your future is blessed. But that is not all. If you are experiencing good things, but the good things don't match up with the God thing (your God-given dream or calling), don't settle. You are in a season and a place to grow. It is a time to learn, to be developed. God will eventually move you.

Many times when God places dreams in us, calls us, anoints us; a significant amount of time transpires between the calling, the anointing, and the fulfillment. I know it isn't popular. I know we don't like it. But often God gives a word—and then we wait.

Do you feel as if much of your life has been comprised of the long haul?

- It's been years since God gave you a word.
- Things didn't go the way you thought they would go.
- There have been some struggles along the way.
- But you've been learning along the way.

Be encouraged—you are learning something that is setting you up for even greater things! Like Paul, you can say, "I thought for sure we were going to die. But I learned to stop relying on myself, and God came through. Now I expect God to come through again and again." (See II Corinthians 1:8–9.)

What are you learning? Ask yourself, "I have been through ________" (fill in the blank), and what lesson can be learned from it?" If you've encountered numerous challenges, can you discern a common thread or recurring theme in your experiences? Consider what skills or abilities you've cultivated during your journey.

Note the following. During a time of difficulty:

- Moses learned to hear God's voice, an essential element in his leading Israel out of Egypt and through the wanderings in the wilderness.
- Israel learned to follow and trust God, which set them up to possess the Promised Land.
- David learned to lead, empowering him to fulfill his anointing to become a king.
- Joseph learned how to administrate and used the skill set for the saving of many.

We don't enjoy going through tough times, but it is in our times of difficulty that we are growing. We've been given dreams. We've been called. We've been anointed. The question is, will we endure? Do we have grit? Will we be persistent?

If you want to be a next-level leader, you are going to have to be resilient; you are going to have to develop some grit. Who knows, it could be that God is allowing you to go through the tough time you are experiencing now because He wants you to advance to another level, one beyond where you are now. And He is simply preparing you for it.

A God Thing Must Remain a God Thing

Make no mistake about it—God is at work in your life. Every aspect, be it rain or sunshine, mountains or valleys, good times or bad, lies within the realm of His control. This doesn't imply that God is the cause of all things. Rather, it signifies that nothing lies beyond His capacity to turn things around, to utilize all things for good. Therefore, as leaders aspiring to the next level, we must exercise caution not to attempt to wrest what is in God's hands into our own. What is divinely orchestrated must remain under divine jurisdiction.

Consider the narrative of Judah's impending liberation after seventy years of captivity. Zerubbabel, appointed as the governor, was entrusted with the task of reconstructing the Temple. Unsurprisingly, challenges arose, including an eighteen-year hiatus in the reconstruction efforts. To rebuild the Temple, the people needed to engage in the labor. But the rebuilding of the Temple would not be a man-thing; it had started as a God-thing, and it would remain a God-thing.

It was God who had foretold the seventy years of bondage and the subsequent rebuilding of the Temple. It was God who influenced the Persian king to permit the return to Jerusalem. It was God who placed the desire within the heart of returning leaders to lead the way. It was God who moved on the prophets Haggai and Zechariah to address the situation.

Most intriguing is the vision Zechariah received, accompanied by two prophetic messages. These messages not only offered clarity to the vision but also encouraged Zerubbabel, the governor. Burdened with the enormity of the task, Zerubbabel needed a reminder that God's work was divinely ordained.

Zechariah 4:7 speaks of a mountain of trouble, perhaps a pile of rubble that would become a plain—level ground. The opposition and difficulties he and the people would face would be defeated. They would overcome spiritual and economic difficulties.

The second prophetic message, found in verses 8–9, offered assurance that Zerubbabel would complete the rebuilding of the Temple.

> Moreover the word of the LORD came unto me, saying, The hands of Zerubbabel have laid the foundation of this house; his hands shall also finish it; and thou shalt know that the LORD of hosts hath sent me unto you. (Zechariah 4:8–9)

Despite Zerubbabel's leadership in the project, however, the completion of the Temple was not contingent on his intellect, skill set, or power. The initial clarification of the vision emphasized it was a God-thing.

> Then he answered and spake unto me, saying, This is the word of the LORD unto Zerubbabel, saying, Not by might, nor by power, but by my spirit, saith the LORD of hosts. (Zechariah 4:6)

The rebuilding of the Temple was undeniably a God-ordained endeavor. While Zerubbabel played a role, it would be accomplished by God's Spirit.

Likewise, as participants in God's work, we engage in various tasks, which often require us to display resilience and grit. It is crucial, however, that we understand that what is divinely orchestrated must stay under divine authority. We play a role and engage in the work, but it is not about us. This is His work. Our resilience and grit, while needed, can never replace the God factor. No wonder the prophetic word included mention of the fact that when Zerubbabel would bring forth the top stone, it would be accompanied by a shout of "Grace, grace to it!" (Zechariah 4:7, NKJV). In other words, "God did it. God did it!"

Conclusion

Israel's long route through the wilderness was the classroom in which they learned dependency on God. The forty years of wandering held purpose—lessons in following, trusting, and building resilience.

Resilience is a vital trait for leaders. It is not just about weathering a storm but about growing stronger through the challenges. Grit, the courage and resolve to endure, complements resilience. It is the perseverance that helps propel leaders forward despite setbacks.

Leadership isn't a sprint but a marathon. Leaders must endure. So whether you find yourself in a season of waiting, facing challenges, or moving piles of rubble, remember that God is at work. Your resilience and grit are shaping you for greater things. Your journey may be long, but as a next-level leader, you are being prepared for the extraordinary.

CHAPTER 3

MANAGE CHAOS

A few years ago, during a season of transition, I found myself struggling to identify the next step. Our lives at the time were a little chaotic. I was starting a nonprofit organization to assist churches and church leaders with leadership coaching and consulting. It was a huge endeavor, one that years later is still in its early stages of growth in comparison to where I believe God wants to take it.

At the same time, I was traveling out of town, preaching, teaching, and helping friends in ministry on various projects, many of which were construction related. Our son had just left home for college, and our daughter was nearing the end of high school. We were attending a new church, trying to establish new friendships, and learning our way around a new town. It seemed we often met ourselves both coming and going.

During this sixteen-month season, I met a friend who was a business consultant. One of his specialties was working with senior leaders in identifying steps of action one could take to move forward with things. He was a godsend. While sitting across from him at lunch, he asked what was going on in my life. As I began to describe it, he interrupted and said, "You sound a little frustrated." I hadn't used those words, but he was right. Chaos without direction can certainly cause frustration. I responded, "I reckon I am." He then said, "Give me a word picture." The following immediately came to mind: "I feel as if I'm five years old. I'm sitting on the floor in my chaotic bedroom, crying. My friends are on the front porch, and my mom is standing in the front doorway telling them I can't go outside and play until I clean my room. The problem is my room is ransacked, and I don't even know where to start."

I'll be forever grateful for what my friend shared with me that day. He said, "Your brain is a tool just as your arm, hand, and fingers are tools. The best way to use your brain is to make sure it is like calm water. If your mind is in a jumble, you will not be able to use it to the best of your ability. You need a system." He then shared with me the basics of a system that I quickly adapted and continue to use, with modification, to this day. (The details of that system are outlined in my book *Rhythm*.)

During periods of chaos and complexity, the responsibility of managing well extends beyond yourself. As a leader, you are tasked with guiding others through such challenging times—times in which others are also grappling with the complexities of chaos. While this may seem daunting, there are actions you can take while navigating through chaos. You don't have to respond as I did in my word picture.

Going to the next level involves, at minimum, a season of chaos; it often involves adapting to constant chaos. A next-level leader is a manager of chaos. The point is, if you don't learn how to handle chaos well, you will struggle. So how does one best handle chaos?

The Butterfly Effect

Consider the breakthrough of Edward Lorenz, a mathematician and meteorologist who conducted research in the early days of the computer. He hoped the new technology would help him develop a model to predict the weather more accurately. To expedite his research (as computers were slow early on), he manually entered data from a previous experiment's printout to replicate the initial conditions. There was an ever-so-slight difference, however. The computer's memory stored six decimal places between each simulation, but the printout showed only three. So instead of entering .506127, he entered .506.

To his surprise, the results were different. Edward described the puzzling numbers as "two random weathers out of a hat." He thoroughly checked the results, peered closely at the input, inspected the computer for a bug, and so on. After several weeks of intense scrutiny, he finally found the cause. It was a small change in the numbers, literally .000127.

In 1972, he presented his findings in a paper titled "Does the Flap of a Butterfly's Wings in Brazil Set Off a Tornado in Texas?" But Lorenz didn't answer the question. He couldn't because it was impossible to know.

There are thousands of variables that could change the outcome. The possibilities are endless. The vast number of variables creates an unlimited number of potential outcomes, thus making the outcome unpredictable.

Many people misunderstand the "butterfly effect," thinking it implies that a small input can result in a significantly larger outcome. This, however, was not Lorenz's point. He showed that small impacts may greatly influence things, but they could also have no effect. Hence, it isn't about the impact; it's about the unpredictability of impact. There is no way of knowing. It is simply too complex and chaotic.

You Can't Control Everything

Chaos theory is the study of apparently random or unpredictable behavior in systems governed by deterministic laws. For example, the ball's movements in a pinball machine are governed by the law of gravity and elastic collisions—things that are both understood—yet the outcome is unpredictable. Hence, the unpredictability of the future means that chaos is certain and has become an integral part of a leader's life.

Unpredictability, however, does not mean one should shut down and do nothing. Quite the contrary. It is in the realm of chaos that next-level leaders can thrive. Consider Uber, an app-based taxi operator, and the more traditional cab services. Most traditional cab services were unprepared to thrive during chaos (upheaval due to fast-paced changes in technology). Thus, Uber and other app-based taxi services like Lyft were able to seize a large share of the market. Similarly, there was a time when Blackberry ruled the market. That is no longer the case. I can't even recall the last time I saw one. Somewhere along the journey its leaders failed to recognize the value of managing chaos or totally mishandled it.

One of the great challenges of most strategic plans is that they are largely based on the past: what worked best, and how can we repeat it with some improvements? But it doesn't work that way. What once worked well may no longer be the best option. Something entirely new may be needed.

What is often missing is keen insight into the future—emerging trends, changes in technology, human behavior, and so on. If you don't think that is chaotic, look at a trends-and-technology timeline map. No wonder many people struggle to make sense of it all!

The point is simple: chaos abounds. But it need not cause debilitating fear. Within the chaos, opportunities abound. "Intelligence is the ability to adapt to change," said Stephen Hawking. What is needed are leaders who can think; leaders who can see things most people miss.

Mario Andretti, winner of the Indianapolis 500, remarked, "If everything seems under control, you're just not going fast enough." To which I would add, "Leading in today's world (whether we like it or not) is like driving a race car." It is impossible to control everything, but that's not the goal of a next-level leader. Next-level leaders don't seek to control chaos, for chaos cannot be tamed. Instead, next-level leaders strive to manage the chaos.

When stepping into the next level of leadership, one should expect things to be abnormal. It is a new thing, and new things take some time to get used to. Higher levels of leadership though, are accompanied by even higher levels of nonconformity. Things don't always work the way you want them to or expect them to. It is often complex, with multiple layers and a variety of factors that are impacting from many different angles. So what should a leader do with the increased level of chaos? Focus on what you can control and accept what you can't.

Focus on What You Can Control

Imagine a target with concentric circles. At the center is the core, which represents what you can control, gradually moving outward to less controllable areas. The idea is to focus your attention and efforts toward the center—where you have the most influence and control—rather than getting distracted by the outer, less controllable factors.

A real-life example could be a student named Robert preparing for exams. Robert can control factors such as his study habits, time management, and seeking help when needed. These aspects are at the center of the target. On the outer rings might be external factors like the difficulty of the exam questions, the behavior of other students, or unexpected interruptions. By focusing on diligent study habits and time management, Robert maximizes control over the outcome, while recognizing and accepting the limits of control over external variables.

As a next-level leader, there will be many things you cannot control. It seems to me that as responsibilities increase, the ability to control everything decreases. Rather than focus on what you cannot control, why not focus on what you can? Here are a few things you can control:

Control Your Thinking

If you think the leaders you most admire don't deal with chaos, then you are sadly mistaken. Leaders deal with messy, difficult things, not static things. Think about it this way: emergency rooms are notorious for being chaotic, but that doesn't mean the doctors and nurses cannot thrive or that wonderful things do not occur. If people were incapable of learning to manage chaos, we would never entrust ourselves into the care of an emergency room staff. Once you understand you may not be able to control chaos but can manage it, the amazing work can occur.

Here are a few things you should consider doing, even in times when it seems everything else is out of control.

1. Put away the thought, *Once things become normal again, I can get some things done*. Instead, think, *What wonderful things can be done now, in the midst of chaos, to move the mission or purpose forward?*

2. Consider narrowing your thinking while at the same time keeping a proper perspective of the bigger picture. Narrowing your thinking means that when dealing with chaos, focus on what matters the most. What is essential? What is most important? What needs to be done now?
3. Don't allow your emotions to control your thinking. Instead, think in ways that control your impulses. Keeping a proper perspective of the bigger picture means that when things are messy (especially during the collision of emerging trends and events, and their impact on people and organizations), you take time to strategize and to develop well-thought-out solutions that often require collaboration with the right people.
4. Cultivate a mindset that seamlessly balances the immediate and future aspects. As a next-level leader, you must hold two seemingly different focuses in your mind at the same time, the immediate and the future, which encompass both leading and learning. Be careful not to become so overly consumed with immediate tasks that you fail to strategize for the future.
5. Seek to provide clarity and direction to those who follow. This will help lessen anxiety as people settle into a "new normal" based on your lead.
6. See the big picture. The bigger picture is most easily seen when a leader observes, listens, and gets input from multiple and diverse perspectives.

Ask yourself, "What might I be missing? What assumptions am I making that might be wrong?"

7. Stay flexible. Even when things appear to be headed in the right direction, they will almost certainly evolve and change.

Orbit Around the Common Purpose and Core Values

The people you lead need clarity; they need to know what to focus on. Consider the value or importance of making the purpose and core values the center. People should not be called to orbit around you. You are not the center. You will never be bigger than the purpose and core values. Instead, use your influence to lead people into following you as you orbit around the common purpose and core values.

What is the common purpose? If you cannot articulate it, how can you expect others to know? Most often, within church circles the purpose is clearly understood. What is not always clearly seen are the core values.

Values act as the underlying principles that form guidelines. Hence, they help maintain consistency across an organization by providing clarity and decision-making criteria. They serve as the "how" through which the vision or purpose is to be fulfilled.

Values are revealed in behaviors. Thus, if you want to know what a person, group, or organization values, look at the behaviors of the person, group, or organization. Unfortunately, too many times personal values take preeminence over group values. This should not be. The goal, however, is not to obliterate personal values; the goal is to connect personal values with the group's values.

Consider a core church value, such as teams, versus a personal value like personal protection ("I will not allow anyone to talk down to me"). While protecting oneself is good, especially if one has experienced abuse at some point in life, being part of a team often involves conflict. If one is not careful, the value of protecting oneself can result in a lack of working well with others, especially during times of conflict. The point isn't that one cannot protect oneself from abuse. The point is that the value of protection shouldn't override the value of serving.

In practical terms, as a leader, you can elevate the significance of teams by underscoring mutual support among members. You can make teams stronger by emphasizing that team members have each other's backs and that the team's unity and strength depend on all the team members being committed to supporting one another. This way, an individual's value of protection fits with the team's focus on helping and supporting one another. As a next-level leader, helping team members connect personal values to team values isn't always easy. It is, however, a worthy endeavor.

Good leaders hold others accountable for the group's values and principles. This may be difficult for some, depending on their personality. It is much easier when it isn't about the leader, what he or she may or may not like or dislike. Instead, it is about the core values. Once a leader understands the importance of helping others align with the group values, it becomes much easier to call others into alignment with them.

Communicate with Assurance and Clarity

In times of unpredictability and complexity, communicate with clarity. People seek assurance, especially amid chaos. Anticipate questions and acknowledge potential doubts. While not everyone may express their feelings, some will. When they do, don't discount their feelings. They are often rooted in fear. Listen closely to what is communicated, but at the same time don't allow fear to drive the organization. Clear communication is needed, so speak up. Moreover, expect the need to over-communicate certain points before they take root. Although a more detailed discussion on communication is reserved for chapter 12, "Practice Active Listening," its role in addressing chaos is noteworthy.

Set Prioritized Goals but Remain Flexible

Chaos causes some to shut down. For others, it can lead to extreme focus, but not always on the right thing. If you don't know what the priority is, you will find yourself spinning.

Consider making a list of ten things you need to get done, things that are on your mind that you know would help move things forward. Do not worry about placing them in order of importance; however, do number the list. Once the list has been created, ask yourself, "Which one should I focus on next: 1 or 2, 1 or 3, 1 or 4"? and so on. Then ask yourself the same thing regarding 2 or 3, 2 or 4, and so on. Continue with the same, ending with 9 or 10. Afterward, add up the number of 1s, 2s, 3s, and so on. The highest-numbered number is your top priority. The second highest is the next top priority and so on. This simple tool is incredibly beneficial in helping people identify their priorities.

A friend of mine had recently started a new church. After going through the prioritizing process, he remarked with a surprised look on his face, "This is amazing! I just discovered that what I have been focusing on for the past five months isn't my top priority. It is number 10. I should have been focused on other things first. I can't believe I just now discovered this."

My minister friend was greatly surprised with the results. You might be too. Leaders often focus on good things at the wrong time during chaotic periods. Make sure you set some goals but remain flexible. Your priorities might need to change.

Handle Challenges with Grace

Chaos is full of challenges. As a next-level leader, especially early on, it can be daunting. A minister friend once described his first six months of next-level responsibility by saying, "I feel as if I've been drinking water from a fire hydrant." I laughed heartily at the word picture, but I fully understood what he meant.

Sometimes the challenges of leading are exceedingly greater than we imagined they would be. We can take consolation, however, in God's words to Paul found in II Corinthians 12:9: "My grace is sufficient for thee: for my strength is made perfect in weakness." God's grace is always more than enough, and it is in our weakness that His power is at its greatest.

It is difficult to pass on to others what we have yet to receive. Challenges can be met gracefully once we understand that we are not fully responsible for making everything happen. We can, however, lean on the One who is more than able. To be clear, we best handle challenges with grace when we embrace our limitations. We don't have to have all the answers all the time. It is okay to be lacking because it is in our infirmities that the power of Christ rests upon us (II Corinthians 12:9).

Set Healthy Boundaries

The phrase "Rome wasn't built in a day" underscores the importance of time in the process of creating remarkable things. We know this to be true, yet we often forsake important things in our attempt to build great things in record time—things like our health, friends, family, and relationship with God. We think, *I don't have time today, but once we get past this challenge, I will have time then.* While we certainly face times of crisis that demand our immediate attention, if we aren't careful, especially when stepping into the next level, it can easily turn into the norm. Hence, next-level leaders must seek to establish healthy boundaries, not for others but for themselves. (Additional information on maintaining healthy boundaries will be covered in chapter 8, "Establish a New Rhythm.")

Conclusion

In essence, when navigating through chaos, leaders must acknowledge the inherent lack of control over the past and future as well as the actions and opinions of others. Chaos is naturally messy and unpredictable, as demonstrated by the butterfly effect. The notion of concentric circles underscores the importance of prioritizing and directing efforts toward actionable elements.

So what can leaders control? They can center their focus around a common purpose and core values, communicate with clarity and assurance amid chaos, and maintain flexibility while prioritizing goals. Ultimately, embracing the realities of what can and cannot be controlled, and directing attention to what can be controlled empowers next-level leaders to effectively navigate through chaos.

CHAPTER 4

DO, BUT DON'T FORSAKE BECOMING

As a teenager, I felt the unmistakable call of God on my life. My dad, who was my pastor, had a broader perspective of ministry than many others. He often remarked on the need for dedicated Christian CPAs. Although I initially aspired to be an attorney, I wanted mostly to fulfill God's call on my life. I just wasn't sure what it would look like. Was I to be an attorney, a CPA, or some other profession?

At fifteen years old, I gained some clarity when I dreamed I was standing behind a pulpit preaching. Soon after, I stepped into the sanctuary of a church I had never visited. I stood there in amazement. Everything in the sanctuary—the color of the pews and carpet, where the plants and musical instruments were placed on the platform, and so on—was identical to my dream. I knew God was confirming His calling in my life; I was going to be a preacher.

I didn't realize the full impact of the moment at the time, but I said, "One day, I will preach in this church. I will preach about Joseph holding on to his dream and how we shouldn't let our dreams die." Years later, during a tumultuous transition in our lives, the church's senior pastor called and asked if I would preach for him that Sunday. It was an exciting moment when my dream became a reality as I stepped behind the pulpit and preached the message God had given me thirty years prior.

At the time of my calling, I did not know of the journey that would follow—the difficulties I would encounter, the trials I would endure, and my faith that would take on an entirely new dimension. I did not know how much I would grow during the years between the dream and its fulfillment. Over a decade later, I am even more amazed at how fast God can speed things up and move a person from the middle place between what He has spoken and its fulfillment. I am living in a reality that is greater than anything I imagined, and I am thankful. The journey was more difficult than I thought it would be, but the blessings are also more fabulous. The journey is well worth it.

Growth Phases

In the 1980s and 1990s, Dr. J. Robert Clinton conducted a research project involving over 1,200 church leaders. He discovered that only one-third of the church leaders finished well. Although Clinton's research is dated, other more current studies support his findings and suggest the problem may be worse than he imagined. Having stumbled upon Clinton's research project, I became intrigued with two questions: (1) what does it mean to finish well, and (2) what is needed to finish well? Along the way, Clinton uncovered six phases of possible growth in the life of a leader.

Clinton's growth list begins with the formative phase. This phase of development is when a person's family heritage, environment, and upbringing shape them into the person God has intended. Even at an early age, our responsiveness to God's shaping influence carries substantial weight for later leadership selection and development. In my own life, I see this stage lasting primarily from infancy until young adulthood.

Stage two is the inner-life growth phase. In this phase, leaders develop a personal relationship with God, even if they have given their lives to Him as children. They learn spiritual disciplines and engage in some area of service. The leader's character develops during this phase, and leadership potential becomes apparent. In my own life, I see this mainly occurring after high school and into my twenties.

Stage three is called the maturing ministry phase. This is where the development of leaders moves them into "doing." They will use a mixture of natural abilities, learned skills, and spiritual gifts to minister to others. It is a time of growth and expansion of influence through ministerial assignments. It is also a time of gaining competence in doing ministry well. Although this stage is meaningful, God does not want a leader to stay here.

Instead, God has more growth in mind. In my life, I see this development phase taking place mainly in my late twenties and thirties and even into my early forties.

It is the fourth phase of growth that I find most interesting. It is called the life maturity phase. Through crisis, isolation, and conflict, the leader experiences a deeper dependency on God and greater intimacy with God. During this phase, the outward signs of success and affirmation received from others must give way to a leader's identity and affirmation in ministry coming from one's calling and relationship with God. In this phase, leaders experience an increase in spiritual authority recognized by others. I experienced this growth phase in my mid-thirties but more so in my forties and fifties.

The fifth phase of growth is convergence. During the convergence phase, God places leaders in roles in which they experience fruitful ministry that flows from a foundation of "being"—from a deep relationship with God. As of this writing, it seems as if I have just recently experienced a measure of the fifth phase of growth.

The last phase is the afterglow. In the afterglow growth phase, leaders enjoy a broad level of influence based on a lifetime of fruitful ministry. Significantly few leaders experience the afterglow.

Every Christian in a leadership role should seriously consider the stages of growth. Doing so and responding appropriately could be the difference between derailing, merely existing, or realizing the full extent of what God intended for them to attain.

The Breakdown in Growth

The timing in which leaders experience the various growth phases varies from person to person. Moving from one stage to another is not like an assembly line; it isn't that precise. There is much overlap. For example, as I have noted in my own life, a leader could simultaneously experience portions of two or more phases. The phases, however, help illustrate the journey of growth experienced by leaders. The growth phases show the breakdown of why many leaders do not finish well, and they offer some understanding of what it means to finish well.

To finish well, leaders must not allow themselves to become stagnant in a particular growth phase. Instead, leaders must constantly be growing. If given enough time, a leader should experience convergence and, to a certain extent, at least some measure of the afterglow.

As you likely noticed, according to Clinton's research, the breakdown in growth for many leaders occurs in the fourth growth phase: life maturity. The question is why.

Becoming

My father often emphasized the concept of *becoming*. When I entered the ministry, he stressed its significance. While listening to young preachers, Dad would often remark, "He preaches beyond his years." This wasn't always a compliment; at times it hinted that the speaker might have borrowed a sermon from a book or the internet; that he relied more on his intellect than ministering from his connection with God.

Yet leadership entails action. Engaging the mind and taking decisive steps are crucial for effective leadership. Leaders must perform with excellence; they must deliver results. Thus, leaders should seek to grow and improve to ensure their actions reflect the best of their abilities. As such, learning from various sources, such as books, podcasts, and videos, is crucial.

But as my dad suggested, leadership consists of more than mere actions. The leader's heart, character, virtues, ethics, and morals significantly impact leadership. This is the essence of the fourth phase—life maturity. It's a transformative period where leaders learn to rely on God more than ever, thus setting them up for the fulfillment of a greater purpose. Therefore, a leader stepping into a role at the next level should prioritize *becoming* rather than merely *doing*.

Three Temptations

The breakdown in transitioning from a focus on *doing* to *being* often stems from leaders succumbing to the three temptations faced by Christ during His time in the wilderness. Examining the first temptation in Matthew 4:3, where the tempter challenged Jesus to turn stones into bread, reveals a common temptation for leaders: seeking validation or affirmation in their actions.

The second temptation, outlined in verses 5–6, involves the devil urging Jesus to cast Himself down from the pinnacle of the Temple, emphasizing the potential approval from others. This highlights the temptation leaders face to act based on external opinions and perceptions.

The third temptation, presented in verse 8, sees the devil offering Jesus all the kingdoms of the world in exchange for worship. Similarly, leaders may be tempted to find validation in their possessions and achievements.

These tests occurred during a period of extreme hunger and isolation, challenging whether Jesus would derive His identity from temporary or eternal Kingdom values. This is what the fourth phase is about: it is our trial, our test. As children of God, our identity is rooted in Him, not in our actions, public opinion, or possessions. Therefore, our primary focus should be on *being*—on who we are in God, surpassing our accomplishments, reputation, and possessions.

Leaders heavily engaged in constant doing and focusing on honing their talents in earlier growth phases encounter a crucial challenge during the life-maturity phase. Unfortunately, many leaders fail to make this essential shift.

The Shift from Doing to Being

Why do so many people struggle to shift from doing to being? The answer is simple: *becoming* is difficult. No one wants to go through tough times. We don't want to hurt or feel pain. No one wants to feel weak and ill-equipped to handle the demands of leading others. Hence, we reject our weaknesses to showcase our strengths.

The fact is we often care more about what people think than what God thinks. The power of Christ, however, cannot rest upon us with such thinking. Instead of glorifying what we can accomplish, like the apostle Paul, we should rejoice in our weaknesses.

In times of turmoil, when it feels as though our world is crumbling and our endurance is being tested, our faith is prompted to transition from striving to create desired outcomes to focusing on what God is doing within. Whereas earlier in our leadership journey, we had more in common with Martha, we are now called upon to embrace the role of Mary—spending time with Jesus. During this shift, our sense of identity transitions from one based on what others think about us to one rooted in God alone.

The struggle in shifting from doing to being is real. Leadership is challenging. Unfortunately, when adding a major ministry-related crisis to the mix, many decide to retire early or leave the ministry altogether. This is unfortunate. Behind the challenge is an invitation to a deeper walk with God. While many leaders plateau, compromise, or drop out of ministry altogether during a significant challenge, others discover newfound energy and life in leadership that flows more from spiritual authority than from a skill set.

Doing and Being in the Life of Moses

Moses' entrance into the world was marked with a sense of destiny. His remarkable deliverance from Pharaoh's death decree showcases God's hand in his life.

Miraculously placed in the royal household of Pharaoh, Moses was afforded the best education available, including how to read and write in multiple languages.

At forty years of age, Moses' life took a drastic turn. Acts 7:23–24 tells the story:

> When he was full forty years old, it came into his heart to visit his brethren the children of Israel. And seeing one of them suffer wrong, he defended him, and avenged him that was oppressed, and smote the Egyptian.

Things did not go as planned, however. Instead of being hailed as a deliverer, Moses was initially met with criticism and faced rejection, prompting him to retreat to Midian, where he spent the next forty years tending sheep.

While this narrative is widely recognized, the distinctions between Moses at the age of forty and his persona four decades later are often overlooked. Consider the contrast: Acts 7:22 highlights, "Moses was learned in all the wisdom of the Egyptians, and was mighty in words and in deeds." It is intriguing that the forty-year-old Moses was eloquent, while the eighty-year-old Moses perceived himself as lacking in speech. At forty, the aspiration to be a deliverer was already ingrained, but by eighty, he harbored doubts about his ability. The pivotal difference appears to lie in the fact that at forty, Moses believed he could manage independently, whereas forty years later, having been stripped of his position, prestige, and power, he found himself wholly reliant on God.

Moses' dependence on God is evident in the following declarations from God to Moses: "But I will be with you" (Exodus 3:12, ESV); "'I AM WHO I AM.' . . . Say this to the people of Israel, 'I AM has sent me to you'" (Exodus 3:14, ESV); "Now therefore go, and I will be with your mouth and teach you what you shall speak" (Exodus 4:12, ESV).

In the years that followed, Moses' dependency on God deepened. This is evidenced by: (1) "the Lord spoke to Moses [in the tent of meeting] face to face, as a man speaks to his friend" (Exodus 33:11, NKJV), and (2) Moses had no interest in moving forward into the Promised Land without the presence of the Lord going with them.

> Then Moses said, "If you don't personally go with us, don't make us leave this place. How will anyone know that you look favorably on me—on me and on your people—if you don't go with us? For your presence among us sets your people and me apart from all other people on the earth." (Exodus 33:15–16, NLT)

In summary, during the first forty years of his life, Moses had yet to experience the intense pain, brokenness, and isolation that would mark the next forty years of his life. Hence, it is doubtful that God would have used him at forty years old in the deliverance of His people from bondage in Egypt. In Numbers 12:3 (ESV), Moses is described as "very meek, more than all the people who were on the face of the earth." His time spent in his desert experience had brought him to such a state of being. Consequently, it was at eighty, when he had lived two-thirds of his life, that Moses was finally ready to fulfill his destiny—that which God had started a long time ago. At this time, Moses stepped into the fifth and sixth phases of growth.

Abide in Me

Jesus declared in John 15:4–8 (ESV),

> Abide in me, and I in you. As the branch cannot bear fruit by itself, unless it abides in the vine, neither can you, unless you abide in me. I am the vine; you are the branches. Whoever abides in me and I in him, he it is that bears much fruit, for apart from me you can do nothing. If anyone does not abide in me he is thrown away like a branch and withers; and the branches are gathered, thrown into the fire, and burned. If you abide in me, and my words abide in you, ask whatever you wish, and it will be done for you. By this my father is glorified, that you bear much fruit and so prove to be my disciples.

Notice fruit-bearing is not dependent upon you and me. Our talent, abilities, skill set, and personality aren't enough to get the job done. It isn't about us; it is about a deep union with the vine. It is from this union that action flows. Our getting things done and producing results depends on our connection with God.

The themes of doing, being, and fruit-bearing are interrelated and found throughout the Bible. Throughout history, human beings have linked the concept of personal fruitfulness to one's level of activity. Scripture, however, reveals an important aspect of fruitfulness that lies beyond the physical product of humanity's labor. In God's kingdom, the intended fruit are such things as righteousness, holiness, love, joy, peace, patience, kindness, goodness, faithfulness, gentleness, self-control, and truth. This kind of fruit is not a product of human effort. It proceeds from an active and growing relationship with God.

Conclusion

As leaders, we are surrounded by an array of tasks. At times, it seems everyone wants or needs something from us, and we must deliver. Things must be done. Action items must be tackled. Things must move forward.

Such is the life of a leader. As next-level leaders, the pressure to perform is at an even greater dimension. At times, it seems as if everyone is watching. Will we succeed? Will we fail? What about the lives of those whom we will affect either way? The pressure mounts. And then, as if there isn't enough going on, a next-level leader must manage personal and family responsibilities with diligence.

But it isn't the doing that causes derailment or a lack of forward progression. Most leadership dropouts, burnouts, and outright failures are caused by the lack of transition from doing to being. For many church leaders, this occurs during their forties and fifties, or like Moses, approximately two-thirds of the way through life. The point is not that leaders should cease doing. As next-level leaders, we will probably do more than we have ever done. The key is to make sure that our doing flows from being or becoming.

Some time ago, during a Sunday night worship service, I found myself in the altar praying, "Lord, whenever I'm in church, I find myself caught up in managing things, taking care of various tasks, ensuring everything is in order. Tonight, even if just for a moment, I desire to do nothing other than worship You." As I worshiped, God spoke to me, asking, "Do you understand the reason for your current position in life?"

Before I could respond, He continued, "Is it due to your education? Your personality? Your connections? Your heritage?"

To each inquiry, I answered, "No, Lord."

Then God asked, "Do you understand you are where you are because I have placed My hand on your life?"

Swiftly, I replied, "Yes, Lord, that's the reason."

He added, "Then why do you lean on your education, personality, connections, and the like?" Concluding His message, God conveyed, "You may find some success relying on those things, but you'll never reach your full potential or go as far as you could unless you rely on Me."

Hence, my resolve. As a next-level leader, I know I will do things. But may my focus never be on *doing* as much as it is on *being*. May I become increasingly reliant on the Lord, and may you do the same.

CHAPTER 5

DEFER AFFIRMATION

I have never felt one ounce of calling to the gift-basket ministry, although I have always enjoyed being on the receiving end, especially when the basket contains some cashews and white chocolate. However, my wife immensely enjoyed creating gift baskets for visiting ministers.

During this period of our lives, I was serving full time as the family pastor, and my wife, Kerri, was working as an elementary teacher's aide. Our two children were involved in activities at the church and school. Kade, our son, had just entered the youth group. Our daughter, Jaelyn, was still in the children's ministry. Besides our busy lives at work and church (Kerri also served as a team member of Family Ministries and was involved in the Music Ministry), we had both returned to school. Kerri was pursuing her BA in psychology. I was studying for my master of arts in human relations.

Kerri usually would ask me to drop off the gift baskets at the hotel where ministerial guests would stay. The hotel was a seventeen-minute drive from where we lived, and it was another twelve-minute drive to the office. While an occasional loss of thirty minutes wasn't that big of a deal, the frequency of the trips was increasing. I was already sleeping less than five hours a night. Spending time driving gift baskets around wasn't something I needed or wanted to do. Even more important, Kerri was experiencing unneeded stress due to all that was happening in her life and was beginning to contemplate ending her studies.

It surprised me the first few times I heard her say, "I think I'm going to drop out of school." Over time, the comment became more frequent. Then one day she announced, "I called the school today and spoke with an academic counselor about my options in suspending or quitting school altogether. I have too much going on."

I said to Kerri, as I had previously, "Why don't you drop out of the music ministry or give up the gift-basket ministry?" She had always resisted the idea, so it was no surprise when she did so again. I wouldn't let it drop, though, as I realized the seriousness of the moment; she had never called the school before.

I asked, "How many people do you think could lead the gift basket ministry?" Her reply was typical of her personality. "How would I ever know something like that?" I pressured her for an answer, but she refused to budge. So I said, "Out of a congregation of over six hundred do you think there might be thirty ladies who could make a gift basket?" I quickly added, "Of course, they would not do it as well as you." She gave me a look that said, "Really?" I finally got her to admit, however, that there might be thirty or so ladies who could oversee the gift-basket ministry.

I then asked, “How many ladies do you think might have a story similar to yours and have the desire to go back to school and study so they can help other ladies walk a journey of inward healing? Do you think there might be two or three?” She agreed there might be two or three ladies.

I pressed on. “Does it feel good when a guest minister says, ‘Thank you for the gift basket? It is one of the best gift baskets I have ever received.’” (Nearly all the guest ministers would make similar comments.) Again, she didn’t want to admit it but finally nodded yes.

I then said, “Now think about this. Can you imagine a day when a minister’s wife hugs you with tears running down her face and says, ‘Thank you for your counsel. You have helped to salvage my marriage and our ministry’?” With tears filling her eyes, she nodded yes.

I then asked, “Has anyone said, ‘Thank you for reading your textbook, writing your paper, and taking your test’?” With a puzzled look, she said, “Of course not.” I responded, “Kerri, you can’t separate the future from the present. Reading your textbooks, writing your papers, and taking your tests are all essential to the future God has planned for you. Don’t settle for a ‘thank you’ for a gift basket that someone else can make. While no one is currently telling you ‘Thank you for your counsel,’ one day they will.” Within days, she stepped back from making gift baskets. (Side note: Kerri continued her education and eventually earned a doctor of education in pastoral care and counseling. Today she regularly counsels ministers' wives.)

This is the background story of a leadership principle I would come to realize later in our journey. Deferred affirmation is essential for next-level leaders. You cannot get to where you need to go without it.

The Danger in Seeking Affirmation

Words of affirmation express validation. They say, "What you do matters. I hear you. I see you. I think of you." Most of us enjoy, appreciate, and are affected by words of affirmation. We need and desire to be validated. Unfortunately, we don't often receive it.

I get it. It's natural to desire affirmation, especially when venturing into new and challenging endeavors.

I often share the story of the time in my midthirties when I was mowing the yard on a Sunday afternoon. To say I was frustrated that day would be an understatement. One could best describe my mood as that of Elijah when he complained he was the only one in the nation who hadn't bowed to Baal when, in fact, thousands had not done so.

I had been serving as pastor of a small church in East Tennessee for three or four years. Typically, I am a very positive person. However, I had developed a negative attitude, erroneously believing I was the only one carrying the load, the only one who cared, the only one who was aligned with the vision, and so on. In frustration, I said, "I don't have to be here. I could be somewhere else. I could be ministering full time. All I want to do is train leaders."

I wasn't expecting it, but the Lord spoke to me and said, "Train them." One would think my reply would have been, "Yea, Lord, thy servant heareth. I will do as Thou hast said." But I did nothing of the sort. Instead, my reply was short and curt. "Yeah, right. We only have four or five people to train." To my surprise, the Lord said, "If you are faithful with small things, I will give you many."

That conversation with God changed my life. Tears started flowing down my face. While mowing the lawn, I made a vow that I would do what God said: train leaders. Today I am living a life that I never would have imagined back then. It is so much bigger. And yet, it is unbelievably aligned with my God-given desire to equip leaders to, in turn, equip others.

Here, however, are some insights I share less often. In the next decade of the journey, with the emphasis on training leaders, I received little affirmation.

I faithfully trained leaders as best as I could in our small congregation. The Lord moved us within just a few years, and I assumed a full-time pastoral position at a growing church. It was a time of learning, mainly through observation, gaining ministerial experience, and, in time, returning to school to pursue grad-level studies.

I did my best to equip others. Occasionally, a few people would remark I should oversee some leaders or work closely in leading some ministers. But other than leading the ministry I had been asked to lead, no other doors opened. While a few people encouraged me to pursue a counseling-related degree, even fewer affirmed my desire to pursue a doctorate in leadership. Furthermore, and perhaps most challenging, was the reality that individuals who had the potential to facilitate opportunities for me to empower others chose to do so for someone else—but not for me. It was a struggle. More than once I thought, *I have committed several years of my life to studies, not counting all the financial commitment, yet I am repeatedly passed over. I have a burning desire to equip leaders, but little opportunity to do so.*

I say these things without malice. I'm thankful for the journey, including the closed doors. I wouldn't trade any of it for a different path. God was in it. My purpose in sharing these things is to showcase that the lack of affirmation regarding the desire God has placed in your heart should not detour you from your commitment to it. If God put the desire in your heart, if God gave you a word, hold on to it. Pursue it. Give yourself to it. God will bring it to pass.

Comparing Ourselves with Others

We should never compare ourselves with others, yet we do so anyway. Sometimes, when comparing ourselves with others, we feel good about ourselves. We think, *Look at how much more I have*, or, *Look at how much farther along the journey I am*, or, __________ (fill in the blank). At other times, comparing ourselves with others causes us to feel bad. We think, *Look at what I am lacking*, or,

They are much farther along the journey than I am. Such thinking is steeped in pride, regardless of the outcome—whether we feel good about ourselves or bad.

A crucial element in your path toward becoming everything God intends for you to be is to avoid comparing yourself to others. Where others are on their journey shouldn't have any bearing on where you are on yours. They aren't headed where you are headed. God has something special in mind just for you.

Likewise, the calendar, which often accompanies your comparing yourself with others, is no reflection of God's commitment to you. If God has spoken, it is done. When comparing yourself to others, you might often think, *Where did I go wrong?* But if you have followed God and allowed Him to direct your steps, you have missed nothing. You must stop comparing yourself with others, and forget about the calendar. Instead, hold on to the promise.

Some years ago, during a transition, I found myself in a holding pattern that lasted a couple years. Thankfully, God sent words of encouragement along the way. On one occasion, a highly respected minister laid his hand on my head while I was kneeling in prayer, and said, "You are in a holding pattern. You have not missed a thing."

A few months later, a friend called me with a similar word. (This friend was unaware of what the minister had said to me.) My friend said, "While praying for you today, I saw a vision of an airplane circling while waiting to land. I felt led to tell you that you have missed nothing. God knows that things on the ground are not right for you to land at this point. It has nothing to do with you."

In total transparency, his words of encouragement helped to sustain me along the journey. They did not eliminate my frustration, though. It was real. I experienced difficulties in keeping my emotions in check. Sometimes I wondered if the holding pattern would ever end. Would I ever get to wherever the Lord was taking me?

I knew the general direction I was headed and understood God was calling me to equip leaders. Furthermore, I was highly committed to it. We had sold our home, resigned from our positions, and moved upstairs into my in-laws' home. At the same time, I began traveling—somewhat as an evangelist but not in the traditional sense. I am more of a teacher, a guy who likes to train leaders.

I did not have a clue how to get to wherever the Lord was leading us. God had called us for a purpose. I didn't have an answer for what that purpose was going to look like. While it appeared that my friends, peers, and fellow workers were excelling, I felt as if I was floundering.

As I write these words, I am torn. Part of me knows it is time to share it; another part wants to delete it. I wonder if I have written enough in describing that season of our lives so that the reader will understand what I am saying. There were some good days while we circled in the holding pattern, and plenty of God moments that sustained us along the way. But it wasn't easy. It was a raw time filled with many struggles. Yet we would not be where we are today without it.

Eventually, things changed for the better. Even then I knew there was more. More to be had. More to experience. The desire God had placed in my heart would be an ongoing journey; hence, the constant need for deferred affirmation. The point is you will never get to where you need to go if you settle for the affirmation you are presently receiving. Instead, you must embrace deferred affirmation.

Can You Trust the Future?

Perhaps this is the big question that haunts us when we are feeling down: "Is what I am reaching for—the dream, the vision, the big picture to which I feel called—the future God has planned for me? Can I trust it? Or is it just something I've conjured in my mind?"

Such questions usually surface when we ask, "How is God going to fulfill His word in my life? And why is it taking so long?" These unanswered questions lead to our doubting if we heard God correctly. Interestingly, neither question is our responsibility. We don't get to decide how God is going to do it nor are we told when He is going to do it. Other than our being diligent with what He has placed within our hands, we have no say in the areas of *how* or *when*.

Expectations

We often imagine how God will fulfill His word in our lives, hoping it will happen soon—but it rarely goes as we expect. His ways differ from ours. His timing is different too.

I used to think the second commandment was the first commandment stated differently; that is, until I took a closer look at it. The first commandment is "Thou shalt have no other gods before me" (Exodus 20:3). The second is "Thou shalt not make unto thee any graven image, or any likeness of any thing that is in heaven above, or that is in the earth beneath, or that is in the water under the earth" (Exodus 20:4). It seemed to me that making and worshiping a graven image would be having another god, which would be breaking the first commandment. But that is not what the Scripture is saying.

In the second commandment, God was saying, "I don't want you to make Me into a graven image. I am bigger than that. I refuse to be confined. I am a God who speaks. I am a God who acts. I am not a god that can be controlled by humankind."

This is, however, exactly what Aaron attempted to do in the making of a golden calf for Israel. The people did not want to hear God speak. They were afraid. They said to Moses, "You talk with God, and when you are done, tell us what He said."

Shortly thereafter, Moses left the camp to spend time with God. When he was gone much longer than the people expected, they didn't know what to do. So they said to Aaron, "Make us gods who shall go before us." When Aaron presented the golden calf to the people, they exclaimed, "O Israel, these are the gods who brought you out of the land of Egypt!" (Exodus 32:4, NLT). While at first it may seem the people deserted the one true God for a lesser god, that would be inaccurate. They were worshiping the same God whom they had worshiped after they crossed over the Red Sea waters. They were not deserting Him; they were attempting to control Him.

We are often guilty of doing the same thing. We expect God to do things a certain way based on our experiences and knowledge. He is bigger than that, though. He is bigger than our knowledge. He is bigger than our experiences. His plans for our future are bigger than we think. His thoughts of us are greater in number than we can fathom, more than the number of grains of sand.

We need not worry about our future; it is secure. His timing is best. He knows what He is doing, and He is faithful in completing what He starts. We must be careful that we don't break the second commandment and create images in our minds that seek to limit God based on our knowledge and experiences.

We Need Patience

Like the children of Israel, we often struggle with doubt. How foolish we are to think that the God who gave us the dream cannot overcome every obstacle in the way of its fulfillment. He is the author and finisher, and not just of our faith. He is the author and finisher of the dreams and callings on our lives. We have a word of assurance, and we can find encouragement in it. Paul wrote in I Thessalonians 5:24 (NKJV) that God calls us, and whatever He calls us to do, He will do it. "He who calls you is faithful, who also will do it."

If we are honest, we will admit we grow impatient in our wait. The writer of the Book of Hebrews acknowledged the struggle when he wrote, "For you have need of endurance, so that after you have done the will of God, you may receive the promise" (Hebrews 10:36, NKJV). The context is this: many Jews who had become Christians were now suffering persecution for their faith. Some were facing the temptation to reverse course to escape the suffering. The writer responded by declaring, "Let us hold fast our confession" (Hebrews 4:14, NKJV). In Hebrews 6:1, he encouraged his readers to "press on to maturity."

The writer made his appeal based on the superiority of Jesus Christ over the old Judaic system. Christ is better than the angels, better than Moses, better than the Aaronic priesthood, and better than the Law. Hence, there is far more to be gained in staying aligned with Christ, despite suffering, than in embracing life's comforts. Living for Jesus Christ might entail suffering, but the blessings far outweigh the struggles. Our waiting is not in vain. Despite the discomfort of waiting, we need not grow weary. Our reward (the fulfillment of what God has placed in our hearts) will be worth the wait.

How does one endure? The writer offers some insight: "Fixing our eyes on Jesus, the author and perfecter of faith . . . consider Him who has endured such hostility by sinners against Himself, so that you will not grow weary and lose heart" (Hebrews 12:2–3, NASB).

The Marshmallow Experiment

In the 1960s, a Stanford professor named Walter Mischel began conducting important psychological studies. He and his team tested hundreds of children, most around the ages of four and five. The experiment involved sitting a child at a table with a marshmallow on a plate. The researcher told the child that he needed to leave the room for a moment, and if the child did not eat the marshmallow while he was gone, when he returned the child would be rewarded with a second marshmallow.

As you might imagine, the recording of what transpired was quite amusing. Some children sat on their hands. Others wiggled and scooted their chairs away from the table. Some smelled the marshmallow and then did their best not to give in to temptation. And others ate it immediately. The researcher was gone for fifteen minutes. Only a few children waited until he returned and were rewarded with a second marshmallow.

Published in 1972, the study became known as "The Marshmallow Experiment." The exciting part of the research, however, came years later.

The Power of Delayed Gratification

As the children grew up, the researchers conducted multiple follow-up studies. What they found was surprising. Those willing to delay gratification ended up having higher SAT scores, lower levels of substance abuse, better responses to stress, and generally better scores in a variety of other life measures.

For over forty years, the researchers followed each child, and those who displayed patience succeeded in whatever capacity they were measuring. Hence, the ability to delay gratification was critical for success in life.

As interesting as that is, yet another question needs to be explored. Did some children naturally have more self-control than others? Or was the ability to delay gratification something that could be developed?

Researchers at the University of Rochester attempted to find out. They replicated the marshmallow experiment but with a twist. They formed two groups of children and exposed the first group to several "unreliable" experiences. For example, some who were given a small box of crayons were promised a bigger box, but the researcher never delivered it. Other children who were given stickers were promised even better ones, but again the researcher never fulfilled the promise. Meanwhile, the children from the second group were promised better crayons and stickers and received them.

They then subjected the children to the marshmallow experiment. The results were as you might imagine. Those from the "unreliable" group had no reason to trust the researchers and didn't wait very long to eat the marshmallow. Meanwhile, children from the "reliable" group displayed much more patience, waiting for an average of four times longer than the first group.

The lesson is obvious. The children's ability to wait was closely related to their experiences and environment. They learned through experience that waiting for gratification was worth it. They also learned that they could wait. Just a few reliable or unreliable experiences were enough to influence their actions in one direction or another.

Conclusion

In conclusion, the journey toward fulfilling God's plan for our lives often involves facing challenges, doubts, and the need for deferred affirmation. We must resist the temptation to seek immediate affirmation; our paths may not align with conventional timelines or expectations. God's ways are higher, His timing is perfect, and our future is secure in His hands.

Scripture is clear: we walk by faith—even while waiting. Such practice of faith allows us to encounter Him in profound and new ways. Going to the next level—experiencing God-enhanced success—largely depends on it. We must learn to wait.

CHAPTER 6

HUMBLE YOURSELF

How do you humble yourself? Have you ever considered the thought? The apostle Peter instructed his readers to take an active role in pursuing humility. "Humble yourselves therefore under the mighty hand of God, that he may exalt you in due time" (I Peter 5:6). James urged his readers to do the same. "Humble yourselves in the sight of the Lord, and he shall lift you up" (James 4:10). Clearly, we are to humble ourselves. But how do we accomplish such a task? What does it look like? Should we wear blue socks with black pants? Mismatch our shoes? Go around with uncombed hair? And once we have humbled ourselves, do we cease being humble? I chuckle as I write: "I've reached my goal of humbling myself. After years of pursuing humility, I am now a humble person." Such thinking defeats the purpose. Yet we are instructed to humble ourselves.

What does "humbling oneself" have to do with a leader going to the next level? Perhaps you are thinking, *I see people all the time who step into new positions who seem to display everything but humility.* If so, you are not alone.

I see it too. Yet I also see that such people will eventually embrace humility, derail, or never reach their God-given potential. The only way to fulfill God's plan for one's life is through humility. There is no other way.

Throughout the years I have been deeply impacted by the need and power of humility. It has intensified in more recent years. On one occasion while reading *Treasures from an Old Book* by Dr. Lorin Bradbury, I was so affected by one of his statements that I copied and pasted it into my calendar to remind myself of it in my daily devotions. The statement was: "Humble yourself, and I will lift you up. I will cause you to excel. Humble yourself and your gift will make room for itself because I have the power to place you in positions you never dreamed were possible."

I know what it's like to feel forgotten. I understand the struggle in waiting. But it is worth it, for I have also experienced being placed in positions I never dreamed possible. There isn't anything like knowing that you didn't network your way to the next level; God placed you there. Such is the life of those who embrace humility.

Perhaps you've felt as if you were laboring somewhere on the backside of a desert, forgotten and unappreciated. You may be involved in ministry, hold a position, and be asked to do various things from time to time. Yet you feel you are not fully aligned with your distinct God-given purpose. You know there is more to be had. You feel it. It follows you everywhere you go. If so, you have likely heard statements similar to this: "You've been in the background, but I will bring you to the forefront. The word I gave you shall come to pass. Trust me."

Such words of encouragement come from the Lord. You can trust that it will come to pass. God will fulfill His word. There is more to be had, but it also requires action on our part. God will lift us, but only if we bow first.

What Is Humility?

As we pursue God's plans, purposes, and promises for our lives, a crucial element comes into focus: humility. The realization that we cannot achieve all God has for us without bowing prompts the question: What exactly is humility?

The word *humility* is rooted in the Latin word *humus,* which means "earth" or "ground," and from the Latin word *humilis* meaning "on the ground." Informal expressions like "down-to-earth" and "having a grounded view" express the root from which the word humility originates. Humility can be viewed as having a grounded view or perspective of oneself and others. We can also view humility as being open to new ideas, having an eagerness to learn from others, seeking advice from others, and desiring feedback from others. Humility is seen in how people treat others, how they view themselves, and how they receive new information.

In the Bible, humility is described as meekness, lowliness, and absence of self. Humility is not merely an outward demeanor; it is a heart attitude. The Greek word translated "humility" in Colossians 3:12 (NKJV) and elsewhere means "lowliness" of mind. It is possible for a person to display outward signs of humility but not possess a heart of humility. This can be referred to as false humility; it is not genuine.

Jesus taught that greatness can only be attained through humility. He also lived it. He displayed humility in washing the disciples' feet. His humility was also revealed in His "becoming obedient to the point of death, even death on a cross" (Philippians 2:8, ESV).

Humility may best be expressed as an absence of self. Such thinking, of course, flies in the face of "know thyself" and "to thine own self be true." Instead of "know thyself," humility, as an absence of self, declares "know thy source." It is through our becoming obedient to the Father and humbling ourselves that we find boldness and ultimate confidence. When it is not about *me*, we can do as Jesus did—take upon ourselves the role of a servant. We can fulfill Paul's exhortation: "Let nothing be done through strife or vainglory; but in lowliness of mind [humility] let each esteem other better than themselves" (Philippians 2:3).

Simon Peter

You can't miss Simon Peter in the four Gospels. He is loud, somewhat obnoxious, and makes outrageous assertions. Humility appears notably absent in his life. An examination of the Scriptures reveals that he consistently led the disciples' lists, seemingly eager to occupy the center stage. In many ways, Simon Peter appears to have been quite likable, yet he also appears to have displayed some rough edges.

Consider the following. In a moment of boldness, he declared his unwavering loyalty to Jesus, vowing to go the distance even unto death. However, a stark contrast unfolded shortly thereafter when the once-confident Peter heatedly denied any association with Jesus to a teenage girl. What drove this inconsistency in Simon Peter's behavior? Was it fear of harm, shame of being associated with a loser, or a quest for approval and validation?

Delving into Peter's character reveals a multifaceted individual—a tough, opinionated owner of a fishing business. Despite moments of courage, such as walking on water or rebuking his Master, the narrative suggests a potential undercurrent of fear. Perhaps his seemingly courageous acts were, in fact, rooted in cowardice. Walking on water, he faltered in fear. His rebukes of Jesus might have been an attempt to distance himself from potential danger. And his brandishing of a sword also signified fear.

What do fear and pride have in common? At first glance, nothing. However, Simon Peter's story intertwines the two. Both traits—self-assured pride and cowardly fear—share a common root: a lack of humility. It is humility that serves as the antidote to these seemingly unconnected yet interconnected aspects of the human experience.

Most interestingly, it is Simon Peter who wrote, "Humble yourselves therefore under the mighty hand of God, that he may exalt you in due time"

(I Peter 5:6). By the time Peter wrote his letter, he had experienced an amazing transformation. It had been approximately thirty years since he boldly claimed he would never deny Christ. You can sense the change in the words he chose in his writing. Words like *submission* and *humility*. Words that were certainly missing in much of his early walk with the Lord.

In his first epistle, the once brash, aggressive person—the loudmouth—exhorted wives to have "the unfading beauty of a gentle and quiet spirit" (I Peter 3:4, NIV) and husbands to treat their wives with consideration and respect (3:7). The man who once sliced the ear off the high priest's servant now advised submission to every government authority (2:13). The man who once opposed Jesus' purpose now upheld Christ's suffering as an ideal (2:21–24).

It would not be a surprise if Simon Peter had an epiphany while writing "Once you were not a people, but now you are the people of God" (I Peter 2:10, NIV). "Once you were not . . . but now you are" could certainly be applied to himself. In I Peter 2:25 (NIV), he stated, "You were like sheep going astray, but now you have returned to the Shepherd and Overseer of your souls," which seems to offer further support for self-reflection. "I once was like . . . but now I am more like the One I follow."

Indeed, the Simon Peter of the Gospels differed from the man who wrote I Peter. Much had changed. He now functioned at a different level. His life was a testimony to those who desired next-level leadership.

James

While the apostle Peter exhibited struggles with humility, James also dealt with issues related to pride. It is important to distinguish James, the author of the Book of James, from James the son of Zebedee, a prominent member of Jesus' inner circle. The author James was none other than the half-brother of Jesus. But being the half-brother of Jesus didn't mean he excelled in humility.

Like Jesus, James grew up in a carpenter's home; yet, like his other brothers, he did not believe Jesus was the Messiah until the conclusion of Christ's earthly ministry. Was it because James struggled with humility? It certainly is a possibility. Humility involves openness to new ideas and a willingness to learn from others. Perhaps some of his struggle with belief was actually a battle with humility. It might have been more about questioning "Who does he think he is?" rather than grappling with the concept of "How could my brother be the Messiah?"

Over time, however, James underwent a transformative journey in his understanding of Jesus. Following the Resurrection, he witnessed an appearance of Jesus (I Corinthians 15:7), participated in the Pentecost event (Acts 1:14), and emerged as a prominent leader in the Jerusalem church throughout much of the Acts narrative (15:13; 21:18). This evolution illustrates not only James's personal growth in faith, but also suggests a profound development in humility as he embraced his role in the early Christian community.

Humility in the Books of James and I Peter

Both James and Peter quoted Proverbs 3:34: "God opposes the proud but gives grace to the humble." Most interesting, however, are the different contexts in which Simon Peter and James address the subject of humility.

James and the Church

James addressed the need for humility among his readers in James 4:6–10. The context reveals that James was addressing conflicts and disputes among the believers:

> But he gives us more grace. That is why Scripture says: "God opposes the proud but shows favor to the humble." Submit yourselves, then, to God. Resist the devil, and he will flee from you. Come near to God and he will come near to you. Wash your hands, you sinners, and purify your hearts, you double-minded. Grieve, mourn and wail. Change your laughter to mourning and your joy to gloom. Humble yourselves before the Lord, and he will lift you up. (James 4:6–10, NIV)

In this context, James was addressing the destructive influence of pride and the necessity of humility in the Christian life. James urged believers to submit to God, resist the devil, and draw near to God through repentance and purification.

The call to "humble yourselves before the Lord" is a central theme in this passage. James emphasized that true transformation and elevation come through humility before God. The context suggests that the lack of humility contributes to conflicts, sin, and doublemindedness among believers. Therefore, James encouraged a genuine humbling of oneself before God as a crucial step toward reconciliation, spiritual growth, and divine favor.

Simon Peter and Society

In a similar vein, Simon Peter addressed the theme of humility. However, the context in I Peter reveals that the challenges were not from within; rather, they stemmed from external sources. Peter highlighted that his readers were undergoing "various trials" (I Peter 1:6, NKJV), facing slander (2:12), and enduring the unjust pains of suffering (2:19). Society was subjecting them to insults, and while their suffering was primarily social and emotional at this point, physical challenges loomed on the horizon. Some were grappling with wavering faith while others were anxious about the extent of their endurance. Notably, Peter himself experienced imprisonment and beatings due to his faith. This certainly would have had some bearing on his readers.

In the face of these trials, Simon Peter encouraged his readers to adopt a posture of humility. Despite the humbling nature of their experiences, Peter advised against a confrontational response to those causing trouble. Instead of asserting themselves defiantly, he urged them to bow down. He assured them that God would provide the grace needed for endurance, but the crucial first step was to clothe themselves with humility (I Peter 5:5). Humility was the foundation upon which they could navigate and withstand the challenges they were facing.

How Do You Humble Yourself?

The pivotal questions in the letters of Peter and James were those of response: When confronted with humbling circumstances, what will you do? Will humility prevail, or will pride dictate your reactions? Will you defiantly raise yourself up, or will you choose the posture of bowing down? Is your trust in God, or will self-reliance take precedence? Are you going to walk in God's ways, or opt for your own path?

"Humble yourself," James exhorted his readers. This echoed Simon Peter's call for humility. Humility is not a skill one teaches oneself nor is it achieved through a twelve-step plan. The Bible illustrates that self-humbling is not an independent endeavor; rather, it is something received, embraced, or welcomed. It involves our response to circumstances and a willingness to accept and embrace God's plan, regardless of the situation.

Similarly, II Chronicles 7 reveals a call for humility. The context reveals, however, that the challenge wasn't from external sources, as in Simon Peter's exhortation to embrace humility. Nor was it internal, as in James's encouragement to embrace humility. Instead, in this context, the challenge was one presented by God Himself. He stated,

> If I shut up heaven that there be no rain, or if I command the locusts to devour the land, or if I send pestilence among my people; if my people, which are called by my name, shall humble themselves, and pray, and seek my face, and turn from their wicked ways; then will I hear from heaven, and will forgive their sin, and will heal their land. (II Chronicles 7:13–14)

In other words, if my people refuse to "bow up" and instead bow down—if they refuse to take matters into their own hands—then I will hear, forgive, and heal.

Yet the underlying question persists: when inevitable trials come, will our response be one of prideful defiance or humble submission? The choice between bowing up with pride and bowing down with humility shapes the trajectory of our journey.

Lifted Up

Interestingly, when exhorting their readers to humble themselves, both Simon Peter and James referred to the humbled person being lifted up. What does this mean?

At first glance, it would seem the Scriptures indicate that the humble person will be the exalted person—that prestige is achieved through the act of humility. Power and great possessions are also a possibility. But that is not what the Scripture is saying.

Consider the following. Jesus was lifted up. Concerning Jesus, Paul wrote, "And being found in fashion as a man, he humbled himself and became obedient unto death, even the death of the cross" (Philippians 2:8). In John 12:32, Jesus, speaking of Himself, said, "And I, if I be lifted up from the earth, will draw all men unto me." Although "being lifted up" in this verse is commonly applied to praise and worship—if we, His people, will praise Him, He will draw people unto Himself—the context reveals that is not so. The next verse declares, "This he said, signifying what death he should die" (John 12:33). Hence, when Jesus spoke of being "lifted up," He was referencing the cross; He was talking about fulfilling His purpose.

Our being lifted up does not mean that through the act of humbling ourselves we will be exalted or that we will obtain prestige. On the contrary, being lifted up signifies the fulfillment of our purpose. Stated differently, our purpose cannot be realized without humility. We might achieve success in the eyes of others, but we won't fulfill our purpose. We might obtain honor, power, and prestige, but if we fail to embrace humility, we will never be what we could have been or achieve what we could have achieved.

Therefore, we must not despise what God uses to accomplish His purposes. Consider Paul. At first, he rejected God's methods. But when he received a revelation, what once had been a source of frustration became his glory point. In II Corinthians 12:7 (NKJV), he acknowledged, "And lest I should be exalted above measure by the abundance of the revelations, a thorn in the flesh was given to me, a messenger of Satan to buffet me, lest I be exalted above measure." Paul went on to declare in verse 9 that he would rather boast in his weaknesses, emphasizing that strength emerges in moments of weakness.

What has God placed or allowed in your life to keep you humble? Is it a physical ailment? A financial problem? Does it have to do with a broken relationship? Perhaps it is something that happened to you as a kid, something you had no power over. Whatever it might be, understand this: God never allows one hurt, one pain, to be wasted. Not when we embrace humility. Through humility, God lifts us up from what otherwise would have been a wasteful experience and causes us to fulfill great and important purposes.

The Water Bottle

I was asked to speak about leadership at a gathering of up-and-coming church leaders. During my preliminary remarks, however, things unraveled, albeit in a good way. The speech I had planned never happened. I never opened my iPad. For the next one and a half hours, it was all simply a move of the Spirit.

Toward the end, I felt inspired to share a simple illustration. I grabbed a water bottle, and holding it out in front of me, I remarked, "The Bible says that if we will humble ourselves under the mighty hand of God . . . [I held the water bottle under my other hand], He will lift us up." I shifted my hand that was hovering over the water bottle to underneath the water bottle and lifted the bottle high in the air. I added while repeating the illustration, "There comes a time in which God shifts His hand and lifts you up."

Immediately, the Lord spoke to me: "You thought the lid to your ministry has been your lack of connections, opportunities, and so on. But it has always been My hand." It was a life-altering moment for me. I also knew what God was saying without Him having to say it. He was going to lift me up.

The Wednesday following, my daughter began sharing with me her subject for speaking to the youth that night—humility. I remarked I was going to be speaking on the same thing to the adults and shared with her the water bottle story that had occurred on Saturday. When I finished, she looked at me and said, "Dad, you need to make sure that you cover what 'lifted up' means. Because it certainly doesn't mean what most people think."

She was right. It doesn't. And I am so thankful it doesn't. Fulfilling God's purpose in one's life is of greater value than things like power, prestige, and so on.

Why Humility Is Essential

What role does humility play in the life of a next-level leader? An indispensable one. Let's look at some possibilities.

Leadership is sometimes perceived as taking charge, in making tough decisions in the face of adversity. At first glance, this might appear incompatible with humility. However, this assumption doesn't always hold. Humility, exemplified by Jesus, is not synonymous with weakness or indecisiveness. In His humility, Jesus exhibited unwavering confidence in His identity. He didn't have an issue in stepping up and stepping out when needed.

In contrast, humility can also be seen in a leader's willingness to embrace vulnerability. Leaders who struggle with vulnerability often project invincibility. But not Jesus. The writer of Hebrews emphasized this, stating, "Though he were a Son, yet learned he obedience by the things which he suffered" (Hebrews 5:8). Jesus' demonstration of vulnerability demanded considerable strength. Likewise, leaders who display vulnerability are often much stronger than others might think.

Equally, when a leader humbly admits a lack of knowledge, it is a sign of strength rather than weakness. Such leadership fosters a culture of learning and establishes an environment conducive to collaboration. The willingness to acknowledge areas of ignorance not only enhances credibility but also fortifies relationships. Hence, leaders who embrace vulnerability find themselves in the optimal position to guide organizations toward success.

Conclusion

In conclusion, the path of humility is a continual transformation rather than a one-time accomplishment.

Embracing humility entails an ongoing commitment to bow down, be vulnerable, and acknowledge one's limitations.

For leaders, the importance of humility cannot be emphasized enough; it serves as a powerful catalyst for success. Leaders who wholeheartedly embrace humility find themselves aligning with God's plans, purposes, and promises. Their openness to vulnerability, acknowledgment of limitations, and collaborative spirit position them as next-level leaders for organizations seeking success.

Humility, far from being merely a desirable quality, is an essential foundation for a next-level leader. Amid challenges and opportunities, the decision between prideful defiance and humble submission profoundly influences the course of our journey. The call to humble ourselves is a call to align with God's plan, to fulfill His purpose in and for our lives. What could be better than that?

CHAPTER 7

EMBRACE LONELINESS

We've heard it said, "It is lonely at the top." The statement implies that those at the top experience loneliness because of the nature of leadership. It is a given, something leaders must deal with. And to a certain extent, it is true. The "top" is typically an uncrowded place. Few understand; few can relate.

Several years ago an elder in my life said something similar: "The higher you go in leadership, the more alone you will find yourself." I asked him why. He replied, "Some people can't handle you being successful. Chalk it up to jealousy. Others will struggle to interact with you, likely because of intimidation. For some, you will just drift apart; your values are taking you in different directions." He was right. There is a measure of loneliness in being a leader.

Just because you may stand alone at the top doesn't mean you are alone in experiencing loneliness. Everyone does. Author Ronald Rolheiser said it well in his book *The Restless Heart*:

> No person has ever walked our earth and been free from the pains of loneliness. Rich and poor, wise and ignorant, faith-filled and agnostic, healthy and unhealthy have all alike had to face and struggle with its potentially paralyzing grip. It has granted no immunities. To be human is to be lonely.

But just because one experiences loneliness does not mean there isn't value to be found in it. A few years after the "it's lonely at the top" conversation, one of my friends remarked that leadership is lonely. He had recently assumed a new leadership role and was struggling with feelings of loneliness. I shared with him what had been shared with me: "It is lonely at the top." But I didn't stop there. "Learn to embrace it," I added. "Lean into it. You will grow from it. And God will bring others into your life. All of it will enrich you." He called me a year later, saying, "You were right. Things are better. I have grown through the experience of being lonely."

It should be noted, however, that although we must embrace loneliness, we should never walk alone. There is nevertheless a measure of loneliness in leading. Let's look at why, what you can do about it, and what you can glean from it.

The Effects of Loneliness

The impact of loneliness is far-reaching. It has been known to affect individuals physically, psychologically, emotionally, and relationally. Young and old, rich and poor, outgoing and introverted are all affected by it. It is a universal human emotion that is both complex and unique to everyone.

In terms of physical health:

1. Loneliness can disrupt sleep patterns leading to sleep-related issues.
2. Loneliness may cause alterations in immune function.
3. Long-term loneliness is connected to high blood pressure.
4. Loneliness may impact cognitive function.

Psychologically:

1. Loneliness is closely linked to mental health issues, with numerous studies highlighting its association with depression and anxiety.
2. Loneliness often leads to a negative self-perception.
3. The impact of loneliness extends to personal relationships.
4. Loneliness can result in social isolation, limiting opportunities for meaningful connections.

While loneliness is often described as a state of solitude or being alone, being alone is not the same as being lonely. Loneliness is a state of mind. Loneliness causes people to feel empty, alone, and unwanted. It causes people to feel bad.

Lonely people often crave human contact; however, their state of mind makes it more difficult to form connections with other people. Lonely people often perceive they have been rejected or abandoned by other people. These negative self-perceptions become self-fulfilling prophecies as lonely people act in ways that suggest to others they want to be left alone, further deepening feelings of loneliness. Lonely people are perceived as less psychologically adjusted, less achieving, and less intellectually competent in relating to others.

In contrast to loneliness, solitude is voluntary. People who enjoy spending time by themselves continue to maintain positive social relationships they can return to when they crave connection. They still spend time with others, but these interactions are balanced with periods alone. Furthermore, solitude has several important mental health benefits, including allowing people to better focus and recharge.

What Causes Loneliness at the Top

What causes loneliness in next-level leaders? At first glance one would readily think that stepping into the next level of leadership would generate happiness. That would be the conventional thought. Goals are being reached. Aspirations are being fulfilled. But for many next-level leaders there is also a tinge of loneliness, and at times, much more. Why?

There are multiple possibilities. Here are a few:

1. Stepping into a new leadership role often involves relocation. This can result in the loss of familiar social connections, contributing to feelings of loneliness.
2. Next-level leaders may find themselves immersed in demanding roles with longer hours, leaving limited time for personal connections.
3. While new leadership roles may offer opportunities for fresh connections, developing deep relationships takes time.
4. Leaders often provide support to their team, but the support is not always reciprocated. This imbalance can lead to feelings of social isolation.
5. Leaders' decisions, especially those that discomfort followers, can create social distancing.
6. The physical distance between the office of a next-level leader and followers can also contribute to social distancing and subsequent feelings of loneliness.

There are other possible causes why next-level leaders might struggle with loneliness. I have shared only a few. I hope they might cause you to consider if any of your actions are contributing to the loneliness you are experiencing. If so, that knowledge alone can cause you to become empowered to do something about it.

You Are Not Alone

Not long ago I came across my final paper for my Personal Development class. At the time it was written, I was an eighteen-year-old freshman. The subject of the paper was loneliness. I was inspired to write it because, to a certain extent, I was dealing with loneliness. The school was in Jackson, Mississippi, a long way from my hometown, a small farming community in Indiana. It was the first time I understood you can be surrounded by people and still feel lonely.

New things, even those things that are exciting, things that cause you to want to embrace change, can lead to loneliness. So can new things that are a "God thing." Just because it may be the will of God and fit within His plans and callings for your life doesn't mean you are automatically exempt from struggles, including dealing with loneliness.

Consider the following biblical characters who struggled with loneliness:

1. Leah faced loneliness as she struggled with unreciprocated love from her husband.
2. Hagar and Ishmael were lonely. They faced isolation and abandonment in the wilderness.
3. Miriam experienced loneliness as she faced criticism and isolation due to her actions.
4. Elijah was lonely. He struggled with isolation, feeling abandoned and defeated after his confrontation with the prophets of Baal.

5. Jeremiah experienced a lengthy period of loneliness as he delivered messages to an unresponsive audience.
6. David experienced deep loneliness, feeling unacknowledged and abandoned.

David expressed his struggles with loneliness in Psalm 142:4 (NKJV). He cried, "Look on my right hand and see, for there is no one who acknowledges me; refuge has failed me; no one cares for my soul."

Jesus experienced loneliness too. Isaiah 53:3 (ESV) records a prophecy concerning the loneliness He would experience: "He was despised and rejected by men, a man of sorrows and acquainted with grief; and as one from whom men hide their faces he was despised, and we esteemed him not."

Last, the most heart-wrenching cry of loneliness came from the lips of Jesus Himself, when He cried out, "My God, my God, why have you forsaken me?" (Mark 15:34, ESV). Jesus can empathize with our pain of loneliness because He experienced it.

Signs of Loneliness in Leaders

Next-level leaders can experience loneliness and not realize it. How is that possible? First, they may sense things are a little out of kilter but cannot identify what exactly is going on. Second, they may attribute feelings of loneliness to something else. Last, they may mask feelings of loneliness by filling up their lives with other things.

The following are some signs that a leader may be experiencing loneliness:

1. Their relationships with family or friends are suffering.
2. For some, being overly connected online is a sure sign they are dealing with feelings of loneliness.
3. Many leaders are overly busy; they never stop. They seek to mask the pain of loneliness with activity. If they stop, they must deal with the feeling of being alone.
4. Many leaders live unhealthy lives—poor eating habits, lack of exercise, little sleep, and so on. Such things can lead to other poor decisions, and loneliness is often a contributing factor.
5. Some are overly driven. The problem isn't being driven; the problem is when being driven leads to loneliness. When achieving success is more important than one's emotional, mental, physical, relational, and spiritual well-being, something is wrong.

There are just a few possible signs of loneliness. As one can see, feelings of loneliness are often masked as something different.

What to Do if You Are Lonely

How should a next-level leader deal with feelings of loneliness? David knew what to do. He turned to God. He wrote in Psalm 25:16–17 (NIV), "Turn to me and be gracious to me, for I am lonely and afflicted. Relieve the troubles of my heart and free me from my anguish." We should do the same.

But what does "turning to God" look like in practical terms for a next-level leader? Consider the following that might prevent or at least minimize negative outcomes associated with loneliness:

1. Foster a deep connection with God.
2. Build meaningful connections with a diverse network of people.
3. Actively participate in ongoing professional development.
4. Prioritize the well-being of both body and mind.
5. Cultivate a circle of confidants, individuals with whom you can share openly and seek support.
6. Embrace authentic leadership by staying true to your values and principles.
7. Engage in the practice of journaling to reflect on experiences, thoughts, and emotions, all of which promote self-awareness.
8. Proactively build and nurture relationships.

Possible ways of addressing loneliness effectively are many. The key is to do something. Next-level leaders must not allow feelings of loneliness to impede their life and progress. Instead, they can do something about it.

Embracing Loneliness

On the other hand, at least to a certain extent, next-level leaders should embrace a measure of loneliness.

To date, I have experienced my deepest feelings of loneliness while being surrounded by people. It took a while before I could identify what I had been feeling. The root cause of my loneliness was that I was in a transition, going to the next level. The senior pastor and I had already had a conversation concerning my future. We both knew I would be leaving. But when and where I would go I didn't have a clue. Things unfolded much more slowly than my wife and I expected. What we thought would only be a four- or five-month process ended up taking nearly two years.

The wait, however, was not a waste. I completed my doctoral studies while fulfilling my responsibilities as a full-time family pastor. At the same time, my wife also completed her master's degree. And we were blessed with wonderful friends and a wonderful church family. Yet I experienced loneliness.

I wondered why. Upon reflection I believe there were several contributing factors, the most important of which was that God was calling me closer to Him. My feelings of loneliness moved me further in that direction, and I experienced some wonderful times with the Lord.

Second, that particular time of loneliness coincided with my aligning with my core values. I didn't set out with an intentional pursuit of my core values; it occurred naturally. As I found myself headed in a different direction than those close to me, I analyzed my situation. I was not better than they were. They were not better than me. I simply had a different set of values. My values were taking me places they were not going. They were and still are great friends. But we have all walked our own paths, and rightly so. It was never easy, and loneliness was associated with the process.

Third, and most obvious, was that I was in a transition, one that would involve my moving away. New friendships would need time to develop.

After having officially resigned from our position as family pastor, the church hosted a going-away service in which they honored us for our nine years of service. They blessed us monetarily and with words of affirmation. We were not sure of the timing of our impending move, but we were ready. All we needed was for our house to sell. Our realtor told us it would sell quickly as we had priced it right, and all the houses in our neighborhood were selling. But God had something else in mind.

For nearly the next two years we experienced another transition. The church experienced great turmoil with an unexpected change in senior leadership. Because we had already resigned, there was little to nothing we could do to be of help to those who were reeling from the news.

It was a trying time, but a blessed one too. Although our house did not sell for nearly two years, God provided time and time again. Due to the nature of the events outside of our control, we started basing out of a church in a nearby town. Our son moved out of state and enrolled in college. I started traveling—helping pastors and churches with various remodeling projects, ministering primarily on the weekends, and conducting leadership seminars.

There is much else that could be said about our experiences during that time. But as to the subject of loneliness, I will sum it up by saying that every member of our family experienced it. But we all grew in our relationship with the Lord. It was the worst of times, but also the best of times. An elder minister, T. F. Tenney, said it well when responding to the following comment I made when he asked me how I was doing. I replied that I hated going through it all, but was thankful to have gleaned so much. In response, he said, "I have often said that there are some experiences I wouldn't trade for a million dollars. But I wouldn't give you a penny to go back through it again." He was right.

People don't enjoy loneliness. It is a bad feeling. But based on my experience, it is a necessary part of going to the next level—a given, so to speak. Good things can come from the things that contribute to feelings of loneliness. Hence, I have learned to lean in and embrace loneliness. I encourage you to do the same. Jesus certainly did. According to Luke 5:16, He would often withdraw to lonely places to pray.

Conclusion

While working on this chapter one morning, I sang the following hymn:

No, never alone,
No, never alone;
He promised never to leave me,
Never to leave me alone:
No, never alone,
No, never alone;
He promised never to leave me,
Never to leave me alone.

Perhaps you are presently experiencing loneliness. If not, you will. But know this: despite the feeling of loneliness, you are never alone. Next-level leadership isn't for the faint of heart. We will experience struggles, but we are never alone.

CHAPTER 8

ESTABLISH A NEW RHYTHM

I thoroughly enjoy fly-fishing for trout. For the past few years I've been fortunate to fish in Alaska, one of my favorite places to do so. I'm in Alaska now. It is early in the morning, and I'm anxious to get started. But before I do, I wanted to take a moment to do some writing. It will be light soon, so I won't write for long as I want to take full advantage of the opportunity to fish.

One thing I enjoy most when fly-fishing is being alone on the river. The sound of rushing water, the beautiful scenery, time spent talking with the Lord, silently singing a song, and thinking about life are all very therapeutic for me. My friends are usually somewhere nearby, either upriver or downriver. We will meet up at some point, and while eating some snacks, we'll share some fishing stories. We will then fish together for a little while before going our separate ways once again. Such are some of my favorite days.

What does fly-fishing have to do with rhythm? More than what people might think. Fly-fishing differs from most other forms of fishing in that the fly fisherman is casting a line, whereas in conventional fishing, the fisherman is casting a lure or bait with a hook, sinker, and bobber. Such things are weighted. A fly, however, doesn't weigh enough for it to be thrown. Hence, the need for the weighted fly line.

In fly-fishing, casting the line involves a distinctive back-and-forth motion. This "loads the rod," which enables the line to extend further in distance. Thus, fly-fishing requires rhythm, and as the distance grows, the rhythm changes. Longer casts demand a slower rhythm, requiring patience and anticipation.

Although I have offered a simple explanation of the need for rhythm in fly-fishing, it is possible you may not understand. You may wonder what exactly "loading the rod" means and so forth. If so, understand this: the aim is not for you to understand the ins and outs of fly-fishing. I have only used it to demonstrate that when you extend yourself by moving to the next level of leadership, you must adapt to a new rhythm.

The Rhythm of Life

Currently, I am at a time in my life in which I am establishing a new rhythm. Things have become increasingly busy over the past few years. This was to be expected because I maintained some of my old responsibilities while assuming new ones. I knew a new rhythm would have to be developed, and it would take some time. I am encouraged in that things are improving. I also take consolation in knowing what changes are needed, and I am determined to make them.

In full transparency, I told my wife and close friends that I have never needed a vacation as much as I needed one during the summer when I was writing this book. Because of things outside of my control, our summer family vacation was intertwined with work. I struggled to get my mind to slow down. Although I enjoyed being with my family—we did some hiking, and I did some fly-fishing—they were experiencing similar circumstances, as they had to focus on schoolwork. Such is life. Thus, this year's vacation wasn't as much of a break as I had hoped it would be. And the importance of slowing down for a few days in Alaska became a premium.

Through the years, both my father and my wife have been most instrumental in helping me understand the value of establishing a new rhythm. In more recent years, a few of my close friends have helped, too, by sharing insights on how best to establish a rhythm and have offered opportunities to get away for a few days of relaxation.

I remember several "rhythm" conversations with my father that took place in my early thirties. Our family was growing—a little boy and a baby girl—and responsibilities at the church coupled with my remodeling business were time-consuming. There was much to be done, and it seemed as if there wasn't enough time to do it.

These conversations would go: "Eugene, have you taken time to spend with your family? Have you taken a day off?" He would suggest, "Why don't you get Kerri and the kids and drive up into the mountains and spend the day with your family?" Likewise, my wife would say from time-to-time, "You need to slow down and spend some time with the kids. They need you." Both my dad and wife were right. Rhythm matters; it matters a great deal.

Rhythm holds immense importance in the life of a leader. Unfortunately, I am aware of multiple stories of derailment because of the lack of rhythm in a leader's life. Perhaps the leaders did not have someone speaking into their life, encouraging them to take a break, to adhere to a new rhythm. Most likely, though, someone was speaking but they chose to ignore their words.

In general, I believe I've managed to establish a healthy rhythm. Yet I acknowledge that I've benefited from others calling me out, providing encouragement, and suggesting innovative approaches to establishing rhythm.

What about you? Is there someone in your life reminding you of the need for rhythm? If so, are you listening?

Rhythm Defined

What exactly is rhythm? Rhythm is the natural flow and pattern of beats, like the steady tempo of a song or the predictable sequence of waves hitting the shore. It's the dance of life's movements, the way things pulse, sway, and repeat. Imagine it as the heartbeat of your day, setting the pace for how you move through moments, creating a melody in the routine. Rhythm is the heartbeat of life's music, as I suggest in my book *Rhythm: Getting Things*

Done When You Have Too Much to Do. Rhythm enables a person to maneuver through the ebbs and flows of life.

While *Rhythm* primarily delved into practical insights and processes to achieve goals, the focus shifts in this chapter. The aim here is to enlighten next-level leaders on the significance of establishing a new rhythm during transitions. Here the emphasis is on avoiding excessive stress during the shift while offering a spectrum of hope, coupled with practical insights on adapting to a fresh beat.

Determining and establishing a rhythm in life is challenging. It often changes the beat—sometimes slower, sometimes faster. Staying on the beat is important. Most of us, however, struggle to adjust accordingly. We know we have to continue moving forward even as things are rapidly changing. We have to get on the beat; we have to figure it out. It takes time. It requires effort. But we have to ascertain rhythm if we are going to achieve longevity and experience significant success.

Embracing fresh rhythms is not just beneficial; it is imperative and nonnegotiable. Solomon's exploration of "time" in Ecclesiastes 3:1–8 vividly underscores the necessity of embracing new rhythms. His insight reveals that God provides distinct rhythms for our lives, each unique yet perfectly suited for its designated time. These variations don't signify a loss of rhythm but rather a simple yet at times complex shift in the beat.

Personal Rhythm

Having defined rhythm as well as underscoring its need, let's look at it in the context of a leader's life. Later, we will consider it within the context of an organization.

What does personal rhythm comprise? Here are a few practical things to consider.

Sabbath

Next-level leaders are busy, especially when stepping into new roles and responsibilities. Often, as it has been in my most recent transition, a next-level leader is juggling multiple things while trying to learn the ropes of the new thing. Taking a complete day off for rest and renewal is difficult, and increasingly so for church leaders.

So how does such a person practice the Sabbath? First, rid yourself of a one-size-fits-all approach to Sabbath-keeping. It doesn't exist. Instead, look for key principles, then figure out how to apply them within your context.

One principle is understanding God's sovereignty. Because He rules over all things, He can make all things work together for our good. He is the difference maker in areas in which we lack. We may feel we have so much that needs to get done that we can't afford to take a day off. When we routinely live with this mindset, we are in essence saying, "God, I don't trust You to make up the difference."

It is also possible that we have taken more upon ourselves than God intended for us to bear. I have struggled at times in being so busy with an array of good things that I don't have time to focus on the best thing. That is not good. Good things must not be allowed to impede you or me from the most important things.

Having stated the above, I also acknowledge that sometimes the ox is in the ditch. Travel schedules, demands outside of our control, crises, and so on can make it difficult to practice the Sabbath. Indeed, times of crisis seem to increase when stepping into the next level.

When faced with such circumstances, here are a few things I have found beneficial. First, I pay attention to my calendar. An occasional crazy schedule isn't as alarming as one in which craziness is becoming routine. I might take a day off during a nontypical time of the week. More often, I will take a half day off. I am also a napper, and unashamedly so. The busier it gets, the more likely I am to be found napping. I have found it energizes me.

I have also made it a practice to pay attention to my body. What I mean by that is I can usually tell when I am hitting a wall. When that happens, I do my best to stop for the day. Typically, this is sometime midafternoon on a day toward the end of the week, and not every week. But when it happens, I stop.

Practicing the Sabbath often looks different from person to person. The key is to cease working. For some, working in the yard is an enjoyable, therapeutic experience. For others, working in the yard is just plain work. As for me, I enjoy writing and often find it to be therapeutic. But if my writing is being driven by the calendar (if I have committed to complete a writing assignment), writing can become work. Hence, writing may or may not be relaxing. It all depends. But I can always tell the difference.

Before our family vacation, I tried repeatedly to write. But nearly every time I tried to do so, it felt like work. I eventually prayed about it and felt led by the Lord not to pick it back up for several weeks until our vacation. Interestingly, one morning while on vacation I picked up my laptop and started writing. It was one of the few times on vacation that I felt like I was truly experiencing a vacation.

I am also of the opinion that practicing the Sabbath involves celebrating the goodness of the Lord. This is more of a mindset than an appointment (as in a Sunday service time). Cultivating a heart of gratitude even amid constant activity is a good and right thing to do, not that one should ever negate the importance of gathering together in corporate worship.

Personal Retreat

I have a friend whose personality differs greatly from mine. I become energized by being with people. But I also receive energy from being alone. My friend receives energy primarily by being alone. People drain him. Hence, my friend's need for a personal retreat is much stronger than mine. Not that I cannot receive benefits from a personal retreat.

I have another friend who for years has built personal retreats into his yearly calendar. He highly encourages others, including me, to set aside time for a personal retreat. Years ago, I planned a three-day retreat for myself. The plan was to go to a hotel and stay for three days. I would shut myself in and do nothing but pray, read, and write. My friend does this a few times a year and loves it. I made it for a day and a half. I needed to interact with people.

I do, however, support what my friend advocates and, in my own way, take part. I receive the benefit from a personal retreat during my fly-fishing trips. For example, while on one of our men's Alaska fishing trips, everyone tried their best to get me to go on an overnight offshore fishing trip. I declined. One man even offered to pay for it. I laughingly told him I would pay him to leave me alone. I ended up with two full days of fly-fishing by myself in Alaska, as well as spending time in the morning and evening by myself writing, praying, and considering the future. It was wonderful.

The point is simple. Consider personal retreats. Don't reject them because of your personality. Figure out a way to make them work for you.

Reflect

The point of a personal retreat isn't simply relaxation. The value is having time to reflect. But reflection doesn't have to occur during a personal retreat. You can set aside time for reflection at nearly any point in time. This is something I do fairly regularly. I cannot run at a high speed all the time. I cannot pour out all the time.

Neither can you. As next-level leaders, we should set a premium on taking time for reflection. We shouldn't get so caught up in doing things and taking care of tasks that we don't take time to reflect on where we are and where we are going.

Ask yourself, What did I learn in the past season? What are my goals for the next season? What has God been speaking to me about? Is there anything I need to change? Scan the past few months and see if you can connect any dots of revelation and understanding. What are your successes and failures with rhythm? How might you adjust to better establish a new rhythm in your life?

Concerning the three temptations Christ faced—the need for control, the need for approval, and the need for security as discussed in chapter 4—which one have you been drawn to most often? Such things can cause a person to get out of rhythm or impede the establishment of a new rhythm.

Last, don't just take part in personal reflection. Reflect on the context of those you lead, the team, and the organization. What are you learning that might help you in establishing a healthy rhythm?

Refocus

It took several years before I finally did what I was told to do. Nearly a decade, to be more precise. I don't know why it took me so long. Perhaps it is because I didn't understand the full value of it. God had spoken by giving me dreams, and I was to back my dreams up by writing them down. I reckon I thought, *I already know what my dreams are. There is no need for me to write them down.*

Through the years, however, I reflected on the instructions I had received. I had also desired to get away and experience a three-day personal retreat, one in which I would engage in prayer and reflection to refocus. When I finally did it, the results were exhilarating even though my retreat lasted only a day and a half. I wrote what God had spoken to me in dreams, in prophetic words, and so on. I wrote out my desires and aspirations, things I had said I wanted to accomplish. Looking at all I had written, I then wrote out ten-year, fifteen-year, twenty-year, and twenty-five-year goals for my life. As of this writing, that three-day retreat occurred six years ago. I can honestly say that as of today I am living out much of what I wrote, and that includes a few things that I thought were nearly impossible. But I had written them down.

Time set aside to refocus is immensely valuable. Your retreat doesn't need to look like my three-day retreat. It could be as simple as setting aside one day a month or a few hours one morning each week. I find value in various approaches.

When refocusing, ask yourself, "Who does God want me to be in this next season of life and leadership?" Write it down. Ask, "What am I doing well? What do I need to change? Where am I headed if I keep doing what I've been doing? What do I need to do differently to get to where I want to go?" These are just a few reflective questions to consider when refocusing.

Sabbatical

In more recent years, talk concerning the need for sabbaticals appears to be increasing. Or maybe it is my stage of life that is causing me to notice it more than before. Likely, it is a little of both. Some advocate and actively take part in a yearly thirty-day sabbatical. Others maintain we need a lengthy break every seven years or once a decade.

In biblical times, sabbaticals were a common experience for the Jews. They occurred every seven years and every fifty years. The purpose was for an extended time of rest and renewal, and they served as a reminder that God would take care of their needs. They only needed to heed His instructions regarding the sabbatical.

Depending on your line of work and stage of life, it may not be possible to take a sabbatical. But then again, maybe the only thing keeping you from participating would be the arguments in your head. If, however, you need to take a sabbatical, you can likely make it happen.

A sabbatical could be as short as three weeks, as long as three months or more. Last, it isn't a vacation per se, which is so active that we need a vacation to rest up from the vacation. It is a deeper kind of renewal.

Here are a few benefits that can be derived from a sabbatical:

1. Renewal. Just as a tired muscle needs rest, leaders require time away to recharge mentally

and emotionally. A sabbatical offers the space for reflection and rejuvenation.

2. Enhanced creativity. Stepping out of the day-to-day grind allows leaders to gain fresh perspectives and encourages innovative thinking. Some of the most groundbreaking ideas come when the mind is at ease.
3. Strategic reflection. A sabbatical provides an ideal opportunity to step back, assess one's course, and align with one's goals. It is a chance to recalibrate and set a clear direction.
4. Improved health. Stress and burnout are common challenges for leaders. Sabbaticals can contribute to better mental and physical health by reducing stress levels and promoting a more balanced lifestyle.

Many leaders have concerns when contemplating a sabbatical, such as:

1. Fear of disconnection. Leaders may worry about losing touch with their teams. However, proper planning, communication, and delegating responsibilities can address this concern.
2. Organizational impact. Some leaders fear their absence might negatively impact the organization. Yet the long-term benefits of a well-utilized sabbatical often far outweigh the short-term challenges.

3. Personal guilt. Leaders may feel guilty about taking time for themselves. Understanding that personal well-being directly correlates with leadership effectiveness can alleviate this guilt.

While such concerns shouldn't be minimized, neither should the value of a sabbatical. Once one's body is finished, one's ministry and leadership have ended. It behooves leaders to manage their health—physical, mental, emotional, and spiritual. To simply say, "I have too much to do," may not be the best approach. Perhaps we should say, "If I am feeling led to do so," or "If those who love me and are for me are encouraging me to do so, then I will strongly consider it and make it a matter of prayer. If indeed I am being compelled to take a sabbatical, I will do my best to make it happen."

Organizational and Operational Rhythm

The focus of this chapter has been on creating rhythm in the life of a next-level leader. And rightfully so, as going to the next level often disrupts rhythm. The same is true for organizations, as a change in leadership is often a leading cause of disruption of rhythm within an organization.

Consider the following:

1. Leadership transitions may introduce uncertainty and chaos within the organization, potentially unsettling the overall stability of the entity.

2. The day-to-day operations and activities essential for progress and productivity could experience challenges that affect the organization's rhythm.
3. Organizational rhythm influences the culture, posing potential challenges to established norms and values.
4. The consistency of organizational rhythm plays a role in talent retention.
5. A well-maintained organizational rhythm is crucial for building and nurturing confidence among the team.
6. Organizations need to be strategically flexible in response to changes, and an understanding of organizational rhythm can guide adjustments to established strategies.

It is easy to see that organizational rhythm matters, and matters a great deal. Hence, next-level leaders must prioritize the impact of organizational and operational rhythm to ensure the sustained health and effectiveness of an organization.

Michael E. Gerber's book *The E Myth* points out the importance of a leader not only working *in* an organization but also *on* it. This involves engaging in visionary planning, strategic decision-making, building robust teams, establishing efficient systems and processes, and more. All of which contribute to and are influenced by organizational rhythm.

Next-level church leaders might struggle with the concept of working *on* the organization since Scripture refers to the church as a body (I Corinthians 12:12–27; Ephesians 4:11–16), not an organization. However, numerous passages emphasize the significance of organizational and operational rhythm. For instance, Acts 6 offers a prime example of the need for and development of operational rhythm within a local church. Once rhythm was established, the church grew.

When seeking to establish a healthy rhythm within an organization, consider such things as the following:

1. Leadership alignment. Ensure that leadership is aligned with the organizational vision and goals. This helps foster a unified direction.
2. Clear communication. Establish transparent and effective communication. This helps to promote understanding and collaboration.
3. Defined roles and responsibilities. Clearly outline roles and responsibilities within the organization. This will help to minimize confusion and enhance efficiency.
4. Continuous evaluation. Implement regular assessments and evaluations. This will help identify areas for improvement.
5. Strategic planning. Engaging in strategic planning will help anticipate future needs and align organizational activities with long-term objectives.

By considering such things, organizations can lay the foundation for a robust and sustainable rhythm conducive to growth and success. The point is simple: Rhythm isn't just a personal thing; we should consider rhythm among teams and throughout organizations.

Conclusion

As a next-level leader navigating your leadership journey, consider this: How you integrate the principles of rhythm into your own life and the organization you lead could very well define your ability to achieve success. Rhythm matters that much. Therefore, what steps will you take to ensure a harmonious blend of personal and operational rhythms?

Leadership is not static; it requires constant adjustment to maintain rhythm. The rhythm you nurture is not merely a reflection of your leadership story; it also holds the power to shape the lives of those you lead, and ultimately exerts a profound influence on the entire organization to which you belong.

CHAPTER 9

LEAD, BUT DON'T WALK ALONE

I called for a meeting with our leadership team, which consisted of myself, my wife, another couple, and one other lady. These were the leaders of a small church with about twenty or so members. The year was 2000, and we were believing God for great things. I gave everyone a three-ring binder highlighting the ten objectives for the next twenty years. The cover on the binder said, "Vision 2020." (You are likely thinking, *Brilliant!* right?) It was one of my first attempts at strategic planning, and it didn't go quite as I had planned.

One of the objectives I explained in detail was for us to launch a kid's church and get Christian business leaders to sponsor it. We would lease a storefront in a nearby strip mall. The services would be geared toward the children but would include family members. I even shared a possible lesson as an example of how the entire family unit would be included in the services. It would be action-packed in a way that both children and adults would enjoy. We would also offer marriage classes, financial peace classes, and so on. These tools and more would be used to minister to families and lead them to Christ.

I am chuckling as I write these things. I was clueless, and yet I have no regrets. I was a dreamer and still am. The world needs men and women who are not afraid to dream, and dream big for that matter. However, as I would come to learn over time, the world also needs "detail people"—people who know how to make dreams become a reality.

I was surrounded by such people at the time, but at that moment I was anything but thankful. I was frustrated. After sharing my grand plan I asked, "So what do you think?" Now mind you, up until that moment I had done all the talking. Not that anyone else didn't have an opinion or a thought. I was doing what I thought was best. I had the vision, and I was sharing it with everyone else. That is all I knew to do. (Later I discovered a more effective approach to sharing a vision: involving others at the infancy of its creation and encouraging them to share their thoughts, pose questions, and contribute to the development of the vision.)

Needless to say, my big dream flopped. Or that's what I thought at the time. After finishing my grand unveiling of the master plan for our church, I asked if anyone had anything they would like to say. One of the members finally spoke up: "I have noticed that when our puppets are speaking (referring to a short period during our Sunday services), we are closing the puppets' mouths when we should be opening them and opening the puppets' mouths when we should be closing them. We should probably start practicing opening and closing the puppets' mouths at the right time."

I was stunned. That was the response to my "Vision 2020"? I didn't say it out loud, but I was thinking, *Are you kidding me? We need to practice opening and closing the puppets' mouths?*

Thirty or so minutes later, as the last person left the meeting, I turned to my wife with a look of dismay and asked, "What is wrong with these people?" (I'm laughing as I type these words.)

Thankfully, the Lord used my wife to speak to me in a way that profoundly impacted me. She said, "Babe, I believe in you. And I believe in the dreams God has given you. Please write them down. Hold on to them. But honey, you are so far out in front of all of us that we can't possibly figure out how to get to where you are. Please come back to where we are and walk with us." In essence, she was saying, "Nothing is wrong with us, but there is something wrong with you."

Together

The nature of leadership invokes images of someone in front leading those who follow behind. Leaders lead and followers follow, right? Such a view of leadership is simple and easily understood. Leadership, however, is more complex than that, as I came to learn. It is a multifaceted concept.

Some think leaders make people do things they do not want to do. While followers are at times reluctant and maybe even resistant, leadership, at its best, seeks to build teams comprised of individuals who share a common objective and are aligned with core values. When such an environment exists, others on the team may lead areas within their expertise. This is where the idea of "lead, but don't walk alone" is easily and readily realized.

As next-level leaders, you should desire to lead but not walk alone. This is the better way of leading as opposed to leading the way while being way out in front. The following are a few things to consider when cultivating an environment of togetherness while leading others.

Rulership or Relationship?

How does a leader lead while bringing others alongside? The answer in a nutshell is found in the word *relationships*. Leadership flows primarily out of relationships. We see this in Paul's relationship with Timothy. Paul did not walk way out in front of Timothy. Instead, he sought to lead by walking alongside or ever-so-slightly in front of him.

Timothy was Paul's son in the gospel. He served as Paul's assistant, but Paul did not treat him as an underling. He taught and mentored him, but he did not lord it over him. Instead, Paul functioned in shared ministry with Timothy (Acts 16:1–5; II Corinthians 1:1; Philippians 1:1; Colossians 1:1; I Thessalonians 1:1). Paul referred to

Timothy as an apostle with him, although he was a subordinate both in spiritual maturity and authority.

Paul's relationship with Timothy illustrates how he could have led without inviting others to walk alongside him. He could have been authoritarian, commanding and ruling over others. He could have walked way out in front of others, but he didn't. Instead, his authority flowed out of a relationship. He didn't demand respect; there was no need to do so. Why would he need to demand something he already had? He didn't have to tell Timothy he was his father; Timothy already considered him his spiritual father.

Notice Paul's leadership with the church of Thessalonica. In his second letter to the church, he commanded and disciplined them. He was authoritative. But that was only after his first letter. In his first letter, he took a different approach. He was first a nursing mother and a pleading father (I Thessalonians 2:7, 11). Paul first had a deeply loving relationship with those who followed him; thus he was able to readjust when needed and give directives effectively. He wasn't always a commanding and disciplining leader. He only functioned as such when needed. It wasn't his norm. Paul's flexibility and the ability to establish a loving relationship before resorting to authority likely contributed to the effectiveness of his leadership within the church at Thessalonica.

Consider the distinction between rulership leadership and relationship leadership. Rulership leadership consists of obtaining the followers' obedience by coercion.

Relationship leadership is based on trust. Creativity is stifled in rulership leadership, as it is top-down. In contrast, creativity thrives in relationship leadership, as multiple voices with diverse perspectives collaborate. Rulership leadership is generally lacking when it comes to developing others, as others are seen as a threat. Relationship leaders mentor others, investing in the growth of followers. Rulership leadership functions within a rigid structure that discourages feedback; relationship leadership encourages open communication. Rulership leadership resists change; relationship leadership embraces adaptability.

There are times in which next-level leaders might need to take a strong stand, to command, to lead authoritatively. However, it shouldn't be the norm. Leaders who inspire through genuine connections surpass those who rely solely on commands. Greater things are accomplished when leadership is characterized by relationship-building. Hence, true leadership isn't just about authority; it's about the ability to guide in a manner that encourages others to join in the journey.

The Right Mindset

As a next-level leader, you should avoid positional thinking. Your position or title shouldn't define your leadership. Leadership is influence. Make it your goal to see the people you lead as teammates. You are working together toward a common goal. They are not working for you as much as they are working alongside you. This does not mean, however, that you can't or shouldn't take the lead. But you don't have to lead in every area.

When leading from a positional mindset, you, as the leader, expect others to do what you tell them to do. After all, you are the leader. The challenge is that while people may do what you say, they will only do what is necessary. In doing only the minimum, followers shortchange the organization and grow disheartened while doing so. In short, leaders demoralize a team when leading from a positional mindset.

While a leader may get others to do things because of the leader's position of power, it is far better to lead in a way that the follower desires to follow. Followers typically want to follow when they feel appreciated and cared for and when their thoughts and opinions matter and are sought after.

Build a Strong Team

Rather than getting people to accomplish what you deem necessary, focus on building a strong team. This is not to say that you don't have to meet crucial deadlines, achieve objectives, and so on; it is simply a matter of focus. Your ultimate aim should be to build a healthy team.

Teams are scalable. You will accomplish more with a team than you could ever achieve alone. Synergy is attainable with teams. It is not a possibility when you are a one-person show. When growth occurs, a team is best positioned to capitalize on it. You can only do so much by yourself. If the job is bigger than you, it will require a team. The point is simple: focus on building a strong team.

What does a strong team consist of? Following are a few things to consider, especially in inviting others to walk alongside you.

Diversity

As a next-level leader, you should surround yourself with people who have different skill sets, experiences, and viewpoints than you. Unity is needed, but unity is only possible due to diversity. There would be no such thing as unity if there was no diversity. Diversity isn't bad, regardless of how difficult it may be to bring people together. It is a good thing. You cannot be everything; you can only be you. Others must be encouraged to excel in their giftedness so the team can thrive.

When team members feel appreciated and safe to be themselves, they are more likely to be motivated and invested in the common purpose. This might take some encouragement on your part. Some might be overly cautious in being themselves due to past experiences in which they were rejected for doing so.

Of course, no one has a right to violate core values, and group norms should be maintained for healthy group dynamics. However, differences among team members shouldn't be suppressed; instead, they should be celebrated. This might entail cultivating an environment in which an understanding and appreciation of differences exist. For example, training in differences in personality traits can be of great value in bringing a team together.

Great leaders don't try to make others think like themselves; instead, they embrace the natural ways team members think and build off their strengths. They know the "default settings" of others by observing what they naturally gravitate toward (and the others don't). But that's not all. They celebrate differences. They see diversity as an asset, not a lability.

Consider the following ways that diversity can prove to be highly beneficial. These are just a few of many.

1. A diverse team brings together individuals with varied skills, experiences, and perspectives. This diversity allows team members to complement each other, filling gaps in expertise and approaching challenges from multiple angles.
2. A diverse team can generate a variety of ideas and approaches that can help spark creativity, leading to innovative solutions.
3. A diverse team, drawing from a range of backgrounds and expertise, is well-equipped to adapt to changing circumstances and navigate complex problems.

Trust

To build a strong team where others walk with you, focus on building trust. Interestingly, the simple act of inviting others to walk with you helps to build trust.

Additionally, respect between the leader and team members is cultivated when others can walk alongside the leader.

When mutual trust exists, feedback and input are easily given and received. Feedback and input demonstrate value and commitment to the purpose and to one another. Synergy is attained in such a collaborative environment.

High levels of trust are the result of healthy communication. Healthy communication is often fostered when individuals involved share common values, have a mutual understanding, and appreciate each other. When there is a commitment to these aspects, it can contribute to a positive and effective communication environment. It isn't easy to trust someone you don't know. Therefore, to increase the level of trust, invest in relationships.

Trust is the glue that holds a team together, and building it requires intentional efforts from leadership. Taking time to know and understand one another's strengths and weaknesses is worthwhile. It does not happen overnight and will require some intentionality, but it will be well worth it. Last, trusting others entails creating a safe environment where others can fail, receive coaching or mentoring, and try again.

Consider the following when building trust.

1. Trust flourishes in an environment of open communication. Leaders who prioritize transparency and honesty build trust by keeping

the team informed about organizational goals, challenges, decisions, and the like.

2. Trust is cultivated when team members deliver on their commitments. Reliability and accountability create a foundation of confidence.
3. Trust is strengthened when team members respect and appreciate each other's differing perspectives.
4. Leaders who demonstrate empathy and understanding help build a culture of trust.
5. Trust is not immune to challenges or conflicts. Effective conflict resolution, however, turns these situations into opportunities for strengthening trust.

Structure

Another critical aspect of leading but not walking alone is structure. This subject matter was also addressed in chapter 3, so it will be lightly addressed here.

A next-level leader must establish clear goals and expectations for the team. Every team member should be aware of their designated role, and there should be a collective understanding of the diverse responsibilities of others on the team. Moreover, everyone needs some understanding of the rationale behind each task or objective. A clear understanding of the purpose behind the actions enhances engagement and fosters commitment toward achieving the shared goals.

When considering the above, it is easy to see that structural issues are a contributing factor as to why some leaders walk alone. When others lack a clear understanding of their role and purpose on the team, leaders are often left with trying to do things by themselves. Unfortunately, some leaders believe the issue is that others don't care. This is seldom the issue.

Be the Example

Leading but not walking alone entails leading by example. As a next-level leader, your actions speak louder than words. If you want others to be committed and invested in the organization's success, you need to demonstrate your own commitment.

Although you may fulfill a different role, that doesn't mean you should act differently. Others do not serve you; they serve the purpose of the organization. To best demonstrate your commitment, don't be afraid to get your hands dirty; don't hesitate to roll up your sleeves.

I once observed a leader give orders to his team but then sit down on a chair and watch everyone do the work he had assigned. There was nothing physically wrong with the leader. He wasn't working on a different project. He hadn't been engaged in physical labor before giving everyone else orders and was thus needing a rest. He just did not want to work. His team lost respect for him. Many ended up quitting. Eventually he grew, but it took some time for him to regain the respect he had lost.

Likewise, while you can rebuild trust, regain influence, and so on, it is taxing. It is far better never to lose it in the first place; thus, a next-level leader will strive for it now.

Conclusion

"I am speaking to someone who will lead people far greater than you," the speaker said. He added, "You will ask, 'Why me?' and it will simply be because God has chosen you." The speaker returned two years later and repeated the same thing while addressing a group of emerging leaders. The Lord spoke to me both times and said, "I am speaking to you."

Today I am living much of that life. I am leading, impacting, and influencing others greater than me. I often ask why. The answer is always the same: it is a God thing. But just because it is a God thing doesn't change the fact that I must lead in such a way that others will want to follow. I must lead by example. I must orbit around the common purpose and core values. Such things are central to what I do. They should be central to all next-level leaders.

Are there areas in which I cannot fully share with others? Are there times in which I must walk alone? Yes, but that is not the norm. Instead, it is an anomaly. While it is necessary from time to time, no leader should embrace it as the common thing. Instead, leaders should strive to do what is necessary to change things, to move away from a leader-centric operation to a team-centric one.

Leading while not walking alone can be a challenging concept for some leaders to put into practice. It requires letting go of some things and trusting others to make decisions. It also means allowing others to make mistakes, helping them grow from the mistakes, and trusting again. Growth doesn't simply occur when a leader tells someone else what to do. Growth occurs when others are allowed to make mistakes and try again.

Leading but not walking alone requires a leader to communicate the vision, establish expectations, and be receptive to feedback and input from team members. When a leader does such things, it empowers the team and creates an environment that inspires others to achieve their goals and drive the organization's success. In such an organization, everyone feels appreciated and encouraged to walk alongside the one they follow.

CHAPTER 10

RELINQUISH CONTROL

We met at a little café. This rising next-level leader was seeking advice as he was about to step into a new role. At the moment he had no way of knowing how soon it would occur. I had some inclinations, but even I could not have imagined how quickly things would transpire or how things would unfold. Needless to say, it was a God thing, as was our conversation that day.

He was very frustrated. This wasn't surprising because his leader was leading from a positional mindset and treated my friend in demeaning ways, albeit not intentionally. He likely didn't even realize he was doing so. It was just his way of leading. He got all of the perks while my friend did most of the work.

After my friend finished sharing his frustrations, I asked, "Do you believe you are where God wants you to be, doing what God wants you to do? He said yes. I then asked, "Is God sovereign? Does God set up kings and kingdoms and take kings and kingdoms down?" He replied yes. I then asked, "So what is the problem?"

Without a moment of hesitation, he reiterated everything: He was upset because his boss wasn't doing right. The way his boss was leading was negatively impacting others within the organization. After he finished, I asked, "Are you doing what God has called you to do? Are you in God's will?" He replied yes. Then I asked, "Is God sovereign? Does God set up kings and kingdoms and take kings and kingdoms down?" He replied yes. I then asked, "So what is the problem?"

He looked at me with a puzzled look. It was evident that he believed I didn't grasp the essence of his words. However, I comprehended them quite clearly, as I had encountered a comparable situation before. I said, "I understand. He's not treating you or those under his leadership properly. He's misusing his position, making him an ineffective leader in this regard. Hopefully, he will undergo personal growth, but you have no control over what he does or does not do. You can only manage your response. Neither can you control God's timing. You can only control yourself."

As I continued, I said something to the effect that, ironically, we get upset and frustrated over things we can't control. There is not much we can do about it other than leave. Find another job. Quit the ministry we are engaged in. Sometimes such things are necessary. But if we think we aren't going to encounter something similar at the new place, we are fooling ourselves. We will encounter difficulties at all levels. Leaders who lead in unhealthy manners will occasionally surface in our lives. It is much better to focus on what we can control and let go of everything else.

"It is not wrong," I said, "for you to see the injustice and think things should be different. It's okay for you to call it what it is: 'It is wrong. It shouldn't be this way.' But when you get done doing that, move on. You can't control what he does."

Last, I added, "If God is big enough to set kings up and take kingdoms down, then don't you think He could make things different? Don't you think He could place you in that leadership position? The fact is, He hasn't. Meanwhile, you are already doing the job, even though you don't have the title or the perks. It will happen, though. Everyone already views you as the leader. You have the influence. The other guy is losing it. Give it some time, and you will have the title and the perks. Just make sure when you do have the title that you don't lead the same way the other guy is leading."

In time, my words proved to be true.

Let Go

Letting go requires work. It is, however, the right thing to do. If you are going to be what God wants you to be and accomplish what He wants you to accomplish, you will have to place your faith in His will. His will includes His timing. You can rest assured that the will of God will be accomplished in His time.

God is all powerful; He can do all things. However, if we place our faith in His ability alone, we will struggle when God doesn't come through as we expect Him to. If we put our faith in His will, regardless of what happens, our faith won't fail us. Jesus demonstrated such faith when He prayed, "Father, if it is Your will, take this cup away from Me; nevertheless not My will, but Yours, be done" (Luke 22:42, NKJV).

Ultimately, there is no man, no woman, no board, no committee, and no one leader who can keep God's will from coming to pass. God looks beyond such challenges and says, "Despite all that everyone else does, I will work in ways that no one ever imagined. My plan and purpose will be accomplished." Thus, when placed in a difficult situation where others are not doing right, we must let go. We cannot allow ourselves to become bitter or tainted due to things out of our control.

Joseph is an excellent example of letting go. He said, "You meant it for harm, but God meant it for good." It is much better to be on God's side and step into the good thing He planned for you than to believe your future has been harmed. Things are never too messed up for God to do His thing. His will shall be accomplished. We must let go.

Letting go, however, should not be seen solely as letting go of things totally outside of your control. Or doing the right thing when you've been done wrong. It is also helpful to let go of some things you can control.

Place yourself in the shoes of my friend's leader—the guy who led from a positional mindset. How would you have led differently? Would your actions have been healthier for all involved? In other words, how would you let go of controlling things? How would you include others in ways that are meaningful to them but might entail you letting go of power?

Relinquishing control is about letting go of the need to be the center. Unfortunately, too many leaders feel they are called to be the center. They are mistaken. Leaders are not the center; the purpose and core values are the center.

What are those values? Do others on the team clearly understand those values? If you can interject values into the group, which ones might you add? Are there ways in which you can include others at a higher measure than you are at the moment? What challenges might you face in letting go of some things you control?

Signs That You May Be a Controlling Leader

Most controlling leaders do not realize they are controlling. And those who do often believe the end justifies the means. They control because they are trying to generate a good result for everyone.

Consider, for example, the idea that the end result—that good thing for the majority—justifies the means of attainment. Such thinking would advocate giving someone a fish instead of teaching them how to fish. After all, teaching someone to fish takes more time and effort than giving someone a fish. They might mess things up, and the leader will have to untangle the line. They might not throw the bait in the proper place. They might spook the fish.

Such thinking fails to see the bigger picture. By not allowing someone to learn to fish, a leader is not only robbing that person of growth, but also stagnating one's own personal growth as well as that of the organization at large. No leader wants that, yet some leaders struggle to let go.

What are some signs that you might be a controlling leader? The following are a few things to consider.

All good ideas come from you.

As a next-level leader, you might be tempted to think the best ideas come from you. After all, you know something about leadership, otherwise you wouldn't have been asked to assume your leadership role. You also might have observed some things that need to be changed within the organization before stepping into your current position. And it is possible you could be right about many of your decisions. If, however, all (or most) of the good ideas come from you, something is amiss.

Consider the fact that the overall health of the organization may suffer unless others are allowed to generate ideas. For instance, the fact that the "good" idea came from you suggests that the possibilities of it being accomplished might suffer. More than having a good idea is required; implementing and executing it must also occur. When others are allowed to have a voice, buy-in occurs.

I vividly recall a time in my late thirties when I and two other leaders crafted a plan of action for our extended team. Thankfully, the senior leadership did not take our recommendation and instill it from the top down. I thought it could have been put into action with a fifteen-minute meeting. Instead, the meeting lasted over three hours as he asked one question after another. I watched in amazement as various members of the team, who were finally allowed to have a voice, helped take the plan to another level. By allowing others to have a voice, the plan became more robust.

As a next-level leader, you need to include others. If team members start apologizing before approaching you with a new idea, act sheepishly around you when their concept differs from yours, or appear timid to share a thought, you might want to assess your leadership style. You might be a controlling leader. Hence, you might be hindering the organization.

You have to be a part of every decision.

Do you think you should be involved in making every decision? Be honest. If you have the feeling, even though you may not act on it, you are likely a controlling leader or, at the minimum, a borderline controlling leader. Does it bother you when you think about others on the team getting credit for something you had no part in?

Think about the decisions that will be made in the next six months. Do you have to sign off on all of them? Will any significant decisions be made that you will not be a part of making? The answers to such questions help to reveal your tendencies—whether or not you may be a controlling leader.

A growing and healthy organization does not need you to be a part of every decision. This does not mean that anyone has a right to make decisions outside of the common purpose as well as decisions that violate the core values. If, however, a decision meets such criteria and fits within the parameters of the organizational structure, must you be a part of it? Can you find better things to do with your time and energy? If so, let it go.

You control information.

You feel the need to govern the flow of information closely. If you don't know everything that is going on, how can you possibly control everything? It could also be that you don't fully trust your team members to make decisions. Hence, if you retain the information, you stifle or control the decisions that are made.

You might also enjoy withholding information. It might make you feel good that you are in a place of power and knowledge while others are left in the dark. This is not to say you are a controlling leader if you do not tell everything. That would be absurd. However, to think that you have to hold on to all or most of the information would be foolish too.

You won't let go of the reins.

Do you fear others being in control of a project? Does it make you nervous? Do you feel the need to step back in and check on things continually? I'm not suggesting a leader delegates and disappears. That's not good leadership either. But if you can never let someone else be the primary leader of a task—if you aren't sometimes the one following—you might be a controlling leader.

Do you struggle with feelings of being outdone by others? Does that fear drive you to maintain a tight grip on all aspects of the team's work? If so, it will ultimately lead to you hindering the growth and development of those you lead, which will result in restricting the organization.

Consequences of Controlling Leadership

A controlling leader impacts an organization, though seldom in a positive way. Here are a few ways in which a controlling leader negatively affects others as well as an organization.

Leaders depart.

Every leader must first be a follower. Furthermore, becoming a leader does not mean that one ceases following. Hence, leaders, to a certain extent, may follow a controlling leader. But only for a short time. Eventually, they will check out.

Leaders need room to breathe. Leaders need space to exceed in the area(s) of their expertise. When leaders feel controlled, it stifles their creativity and drains their energy.

In contrast to a controlling leader, a healthy leader invites other leaders to step into their uniqueness. They welcome differences in personalities, skill sets, and opinions. They do not seek to control them. Instead, they are encouraged to grow, thrive, and excel.

As a next-level leader, aim to identify leaders, current and emerging, and offer them a place on the team to be who they are meant to be. Ensure they are committed and following through in orbiting around the organization's shared purpose and core values. Such leaders will help your team to exceed its goals and objectives. Some will eventually move on, but other leaders will want to join the team as they will see it as a place that welcomes true leaders. This is the environment and culture you want to create. One that helps leaders grow.

Followers become stagnant.

On the flip side, in environments where the leader exercises strict control, followers may remain in a passive state. While having followers who stay may initially seem desirable for leaders, it is crucial to distinguish between mere compliance and active collaboration. Followers who merely adhere to instructions without full and active engagement are passive implementers.

Collaborative followers, on the other hand, play a dynamic role. They ask questions, challenge established processes, and demonstrate a genuine commitment to the shared vision through their actions. These individuals may express diverse opinions but remain steadfastly dedicated to the overarching purpose and core values of the team or organization. Collaborative followers represent the highest quality of followership.

They may prefer followers who are compliant, hesitant to voice dissent or challenge the status quo. Some followers adhere out of loyalty or a sense of duty, while others may do so out of fear. Fear keeps them from going elsewhere. Fear of the unknown. Fear of upsetting the cart. Sadly, such people often live unfulfilled lives and experience great dissatisfaction.

Some years ago when stepping into a new role and responsibility, I said to the leader who had asked me to join the team: "I am honored that you would ask me to join. However, I am at a stage in my life where I no longer want to walk behind a leader; I want to walk alongside. I want not only the freedom to disagree, but I also want to be invited and encouraged to do so. However, having stated that, I highly respect you as the leader. I will never disagree with you in public. Furthermore, I will support you in whatever you decide. I just want to be a partner, not an implementer." I was committing to the overarching purpose and aligning with the organization's values.

Having said that, I would have never thought of doing something of the sort as a young man. But I had entered a different life stage, and my understanding had grown. I was immensely blessed when the senior leader responded, "That is why I am asking you to join the team. I want you to walk alongside me." He became one of my closest friends. He has my utmost respect. He is a great leader.

The organization suffers.

The real detriment of controlling leadership is that it limits the organization to one leader's strengths, dreams, visions, and abilities. As great as a controlling leader may be, a single vision will never be as robust as a shared vision. One person's greatest dream will never be as great as the one in which others contribute to. As great as one person's abilities may be, the organization suffers if others are not allowed to tap into the depths of their abilities too.

This is not to say that strong leaders cannot thrive or that strong leaders must become passive leaders, for that would harm an organization too. In much of today's world, the need for a strong leader has never been more evident. However, strong leadership is different from controlling leadership. A leader can be a strong leader and still include others. One can be a strong leader and still create a safe place for others to express opinions and challenge processes. One person can only control so much. It's a key reason why churches plateau and businesses become stagnant.

Delegation and Empowerment

Next-level leaders do well in understanding the difference between delegation and empowerment, and exercising both at the appropriate time. When delegating something, a leader often hands off a task with parameters as to how and when it should be completed. Conversely, when empowering someone, a leader essentially gives a person the freedom to lead to the best of one's ability.

Understand what empowerment is and isn't. Simply creating the conditions for an individual to take broader responsibility isn't empowerment. Neither is allowing someone to participate more widely in decision-making. Nor does giving someone more independence and influence constitute empowerment. True empowerment invokes a higher level of trust than simply delegating something. Such trust takes time to build. Honest and open communication is a must. But such trust and true empowerment can be had.

A next-level leader should strive to invoke both delegation and empowerment. Delegation is not wrong; it is necessary. However, much more can be achieved through empowerment. More leaders will stay. The organization will be enhanced. Such is the nature of empowerment.

If such thinking bothers you and causes you to question how accountability can be had, seek to understand the value and importance of orbiting around a common purpose and core values rather than a person or position.

Conclusion

Perhaps you're thinking, *I'm someone who puts the purpose at the center*. If so, ask yourself, "Do I forget that people are the underlining of every purpose?" Or you may think that as long as the purpose is fulfilled, how it happens doesn't matter. Hence, you hold on to control. You would rather do things yourself than take the time needed to include others in a way that brings them alongside as opposed to you driving them.

Or you may be driven by a need to keep things in order. You don't like surprises. You don't like dealing with issues. If so, you might think, *If I let go of too much power, someone isn't going to do things the way I want them done, and I will have to either live with a mess or fix it. Hence, I stand a chance of being unable to fulfill the purpose. I can't live with that thought, so I seek to control. It is my best chance of success.*

If such thoughts echo within you, consider the limitations you are placing on the organization you lead. Is that the kind of leader you want to be? If not, then seek to change. Let go.

CHAPTER 11

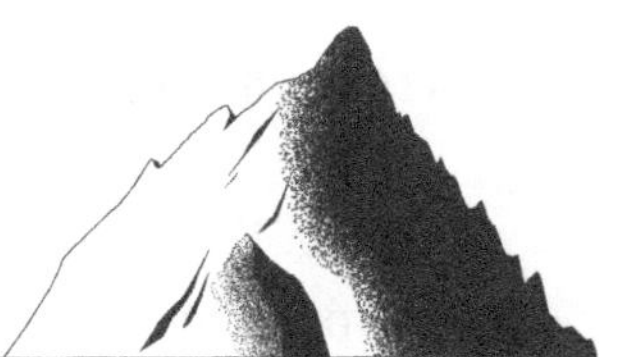

DON'T CRUSH THE CRITICS

I was a young leader and had just assumed the role and responsibilities of a pastor. Filled with zeal, I was ready to make the changes necessary to accomplish our purpose. But not everyone wanted to change, and I certainly did not handle things as well as I would address them now.

I vividly recall a short conversation right outside the sanctuary. It was mostly one-sided, as I didn't know how to respond to criticism. Shortly thereafter I received a phone call from someone else in the church who asked for a meeting. When I inquired about the subject matter, the woman said, "There are several of us who want to talk with you about some things we don't like." I knew change had likely ruffled some feathers, but I was doing what I believed was best for the church. The honeymoon season had ended, and the level at which I received criticism picked up.

I don't want to paint a negative picture. Some wonderful things were happening at the same time. But it was an up-and-down phenomenon that was both exciting and draining. We moved forward two or three steps while taking two or three steps backward. It was a time of learning, a time of personal growth.

Within a year or so of that initial criticism, desiring to be the best leader possible, I did something I had never done before: I sought out criticism. I asked those close to me what I needed to do to be a better leader. I asked my wife, my assistant pastor, and my dad, who was my pastor. I also asked a close friend who had started a church about an hour away. I asked them to be open and honest with me. Regardless of how much it might hurt, I was determined to be a better leader. I needed to know where I needed to grow. What were my blind spots? What was I missing?

The experience was so helpful that I determined to do it again. Approximately every year and a half, I would ask those close to me what I needed to do to improve. The subject matter varied, but the desire to grow did not. Neither did one of the methods for growth—my willingness to accept criticism. I needed it, and I asked for it.

Looking back, I can see I was influenced by a book called *Coping with Criticism*. Amazingly, I can recall the book title (there are few book titles I can remember from that long ago). It was revolutionary the first time I read it as a teenager. Peer pressure was real, but so was the desire to be all that God meant for me to be. Early on, I learned that God could use the things we go through to help us grow, to become what He meant for us to be. Or things can cause us to become bitter. Bitter or better, it is a choice we get to make, and I made it; I wanted to be better.

You Will Be Criticized

Leadership isn't a popularity contest where the goal is to win universal approval. No matter a leader's efforts, it is impossible to please everyone. If you are serving in a leadership capacity, criticism comes with the territory—it's part of the job. Leadership is about doing what is right for the organization regardless of the potential consequences. Leading based solely on the majority's preferences will leave the minority dissatisfied. It might also lead the organization where it shouldn't go.

Even if you reach the top, criticism will follow. Some critics may argue that you haven't earned the right to be there. Although you might be doing an excellent job, criticism will persist. Success won't shield you from scrutiny. People will analyze your decisions and often contemplate how they would have done things differently. Some might express their opinions directly. Others will share their thoughts with someone else. In many cases, they will simply keep their thoughts to themselves.

Having such ideas is normal; it is a part of leadership. I've encouraged aspiring leaders to constantly assess and think about how they would approach things differently. While doing so, I've also emphasized that while they might speculate, they may not know all the particulars. With additional information, their opinions might change. I also remind them of the need to stay humble. It is one thing to analyze leaders and how they lead; it's another thing to develop a better-than-they attitude. Last, I encourage them to extend grace to the leader, as they themselves will likely need it one day.

The Value of Criticism

Most people would agree that criticism is seldom enjoyable, if ever. It doesn't matter who the messenger is—whether it's one's spouse, close friend, business colleague, neighbor, or stranger, criticism often causes feelings of resistance. No one likes to be criticized. Yet criticism can be beneficial, and much of the benefit depends on the one receiving it. Will they allow it to make them better, or will they reject it?

Rather than trying to eliminate criticism, develop yourself until you come to appreciate it. Proverbs 28:23 (NLT) states, "In the end, people appreciate honest criticism far more than flattery." Swallowing our pride is never easy. It is challenging to hear someone point out the areas where we might need to improve. Wise leaders, however, will sift through what is being said and grab hold of a golden nugget that will help them become better leaders. Being able to glean from criticism is a sign of a growing, emotionally healthy leader.

Consider a professional sports player. Few demonstrate as much resolve as professional sports players; they routinely face criticism from opposing fans. But that's not all. Coaches, managers, front office, and even team members are crucial to helping a player achieve full potential.

And it is often accomplished through criticism. Great players thrive on criticism. They use it as a motivating force. It doesn't limit them. It propels them. Next-level leaders use criticism to do the same.

Criticism is a tool that, if embraced, can help you grow. Feedback can be a valuable learning opportunity. No leader is perfect. Being open-minded enough to discover the golden nuggets (growth opportunities) will enhance your success, enabling you to step into the next level of leadership when the time comes.

How to Properly Handle Criticism

1. Don't play the victim. One of the worst things you can do when receiving criticism is to take on a woe-is-me attitude. People will lose respect for you. When leaders play the role of a victim, it exposes their lack of maturity. While you may be young and lack experience, you can grow immensely in the eyes of those you lead by handling criticism correctly. Playing the victim is never the best way to take criticism. If you act defensively, you likely will diminish your level of influence with others, even those who might agree with you.

2. Don't react impulsively. One way to counteract a rash response is to spend a little extra time to evaluate the situation before responding. Be patient. You don't have to respond immediately, even though you may want to.

Those who respond impulsively are often those who struggle with insecurities. Adversity (dealing with criticism is part of adversity) reveals a person. It may or may not benefit a person, but it will almost always indicate the type of person one is.

Instead of a quick response, offer a counterstatement that buys you some time. Try saying, "That is an interesting viewpoint. Let me think about it, and I will reply." Or, "I've never thought of it that way. I will have to think about that some more." You can deal with the things that need to be dealt with later in the day, later in the week, later after you've cooled down and had time to think.

3. Don't take it personally. Distinguish criticism aimed at your role from criticism directed at you as an individual. As a leader, understand that your role and responsibilities are components of your professional identity, not your entire being. Maintaining clarity between your role and who you are prevents you from internalizing criticism that was never intended to be personal.

When you allow criticism to affect you on a personal level, it complicates your ability to maintain objectivity in handling business affairs. By reframing criticism as feedback on your role rather than an attack on your character, you can better separate yourself emotionally from the business challenges.

4. Listen, but also seek to understand. One of the most important qualities of leadership is being a good listener. Listening while being criticized is difficult but necessary nonetheless. Some leaders might be tempted to turn the criticism around on the person speaking up. However, viewing it as an opportunity to learn from someone else is far better.

Interestingly, most followers feel leaders need to offer more valuable feedback. Thus, when receiving criticism from a follower, getting to the heart of the matter is essential. What is the follower trying to say? Ask, "Can you give me a specific example of what you're talking about?" The goal isn't to excuse away what may or may not have happened. The goal is to gain understanding.

Even when criticism is mostly unwarranted, it does not mean you cannot learn something. Ask yourself, "What lesson(s) can I glean from this experience?" You might be surprised at the insights you might gather.

5. Avoid making excuses. When being criticized, seek to avoid making excuses. It is not the time to shift blame or rationalize your behavior. Instead, simply reply, "Thank you for your feedback." Or, "Thank you. I will give it some thought." If you make excuses or shift blame, you will come across as looking weak and defensive. You will not come across as being responsible or willing to learn. None of these are good traits for a next-level leader.

6. Don't get caught up with what is and isn't fair. If you are looking for what is fair, reconsider being a leader. You likely need a better idea of what leadership entails. There are many things in leading others that aren't fair. When things go wrong—and they will—you will likely be on the receiving end of some criticism.

Sometimes you will be the person responsible. Other times, what went wrong was outside your responsibility or control. That doesn't mean you will be exempt. You might be criticized simply because you are the leader, not because you are responsible for the issue. When this happens, avoid getting sidetracked. Stay focused. You will likely be scrutinized when things are not going well for an organization simply because you are a leader. It is part of the job, even though it may not be fair.

7. *Resist becoming callous.* One challenge in dealing with criticism is becoming callous. Criticism can be painful, especially for a leader who is thin-skinned. A thin-skinned leader will need help to lead effectively. The same is true for the leader who is thick-skinned. Callous leaders tend not to listen to others, missing out on the value criticism may offer. When the heart of a leader is disengaged, the hands of a leader are likely to cause damage. Leading effectively requires a leader to be able to feel.

Dealing with Widespread Public Criticism

In recent years, a surge of public criticism of leaders has emerged. This has been propelled largely through social media. This platform provides individuals with the avenue to express opinions, often more harshly than they might in person. Such criticism can be challenging for leaders, as it has the potential to spread rapidly and affect a large number of people. While some criticisms may be valid, leaders frequently find themselves facing unwarranted backlash for issues beyond their control.

Confronted with such challenges where control is limited, leaders can always exercise control over how they process and respond. Consider the following:

1. Stay calm. Process the criticism before deciding on a response.
2. Align with values. Respond in alignment with your core values and principles.
3. Choose your battles. Not every criticism needs a response. Address issues that truly merit attention.
4. Refrain from personal attacks. Focus on the issues at hand.
5. Engage privately. If appropriate, encourage individuals with valid concerns to discuss the matter privately.
6. Engage constructively. If a public response is warranted, consider acknowledging the concern(s), and communicate plans or actions to address them.
7. Monitor and moderate. If deciding not to respond, keep a close eye on the conversation. You might also consider moderating comments if they become harmful.

Remember that facing public criticism is part of leadership, especially in the digital age. Leaders should use these moments as opportunities for reflection and improvement. It might also offer a golden opportunity to demonstrate and further develop resilience and grit.

Beware of Flattery

Flattery, in many ways, can be considered the opposite of excessive or unwarranted criticism, yet it can be equally or even more damaging. Socrates said, "Think not those faithful who praise thy words and actions but those who kindly reprove thy faults." While no one likes criticism, good can be gleaned from it. Flattery, on the other hand, can generate much harm.

Flattery has the potential to distort a leader's perception of reality. If used manipulatively or excessively, it can create a false sense of accomplishment, potentially leading to complacency or a lack of self-awareness. Thus, leaders must be mentally tough to withstand criticism, but they must also be cautious in succumbing to flattery.

Consider the scenario where, as a leader, you believe it is necessary to navigate a path that causes discomfort for your team. Well-intentioned followers may attempt to influence you through flattery to steer you in a different direction. If you think this isn't a possibility, you might be surprised. Caving in to flattery from resistant followers has been identified as a contributing factor in the dismissal of underperforming CEOs who struggled to enforce essential changes and address underperformance.

Looking for some advice on overcoming flattery? One of the ways to overcome flattery is to seek out the opinions of people who disagree with you. In other words, one of the ways to overcome flattery is to embrace criticism.

Forget Yourself

The best way to handle criticism as well as flattery is to forget yourself. This is what the apostle Paul advocated when he wrote:

> But with me, it is a very small thing that I should be judged by you or by any human court. In fact, I do not even judge myself. For I am not aware of anything against myself, but I am not thereby acquitted. It is the Lord who judges me. (I Corinthians 4:3–4, ESV)

In these verses, Paul emphasized that he did not overly concern himself with the judgment of others or even his own self-evaluation. Instead, he deferred to the ultimate judgment of the Lord. This reflects a perspective of humility and a focus on a higher purpose beyond personal reputation.

In *The Freedom of Self-Forgetfulness*, Tim Keller elaborated on Paul's writings when he stated that the "self-forgetful person would never be hurt particularly badly by criticism." He went on to state,

> It would not devastate them, it would not keep them up late, it would not bother them. Why? Because a person who is devastated by criticism is putting too much value on what other people think, on other people's opinions. The world tells the person who is thin-skinned and

> devastated by criticism to deal with it by saying, "Who cares what they think? I know what I think. Who cares what the rabble thinks? It doesn't bother me." People are either devastated by criticism—or they are not devastated by criticism because they do not listen to it. They will not listen to it or learn from it because they do not care about it. They know who they are and what they think. In other words, our only solution to low self-esteem is pride. But that is no solution. Both low self-esteem and pride are horrible nuisances to our own future and to everyone around us.

Next-level leaders handle criticism properly. They listen to it, viewing it as an opportunity to grow, learn, and inspire positive change. They don't automatically reject it, develop hardness toward it, or fail to learn from it.

Conclusion

When stepping into new positions, expect to be criticized. When making difficult decisions, expect to be criticized. When navigating change, expect to be criticized. But don't let criticism discourage you. Eleanor Roosevelt has been quoted as stating, "Do what you feel in your heart to be right—for you'll be criticized anyway." It is a part of leadership. There is nothing you can do about it. Learn how to glean from it, and you will go farther than you would have without it.

CHAPTER 12

PRACTICE ACTIVE LISTENING

From time to time I hear the statement, "We must get better at our communication." I usually agree. We can all do a better job at communicating. As the adage goes, "Communicate. Communicate. Communicate. And when you think you've said it all, say it again." That is frequently correct. The repetition of a message is often a necessity, as some messages require multiple iterations to truly resonate.

Most people would agree that breakdowns in communication cause issues, problems that wouldn't exist if someone had done a better job of communicating. Communication, however, consists of more than telling someone something. It entails more than the words a person speaks or the messages a person sends via text, email, or social media posts. Communication also involves listening.

Listening Matters

Consider this: according to research, we spend around 70 to 80 percent of our waking hours in some form of communication. Within this span, the average person devotes 9 percent of waking time to writing, 16 percent to reading, 30 percent to speaking, and 45 percent to listening. Astonishingly, fewer than 5 percent of people have ever received training on how to listen, yet listening is the most significant component of communication.

Our lack of training contributes to our inability to be effective listeners. According to research, we typically comprehend and retain only about one-fourth of what we hear. Based on personal experience, that percentage likely is generous. On top of that, it appears we purposefully fill our lives with noise pollution—for example, notifications on our computers and phones, on which we continue to add various apps and services, presumably to better our lives. Whether it's working is debatable, especially when considering our issues with listening.

The good news is we are not stuck as we are. We can improve. We can get better at listening. A revealing experiment with students conducted in Minneapolis by Ralph Nichols underscores the developmental path of listening skills. (See *The Plateau Effect* by Bob Sullivan and Hugh Thompson.) In the early grades, an impressive 90 percent of students were attentive and engaged. However, this percentage dwindled as they progressed through higher grades, dwindling to a mere 28 percent in high school. This speaks volumes about the need for improved communication at all levels. Success at the next level of leadership hinges significantly on mastering this skill. Effective communication is a two-way street. Next-level leaders must prioritize listening.

The Book of Proverbs contrasts the fool's constant noise with the quietness of the wise. It isn't that the wise never speak; the distinction is that fools never listen. A fool doesn't know when to shut up, slow down, or maintain a quiet spirit. A fool can't keep his mouth shut.

In contrast, wise people know when to speak up and when to be silent. They are not driven to say everything that comes to mind. Just because they may think it, doesn't mean they have to say it. Wise or prudent people are respected. When they do speak, others listen. That is, unless the listener is a fool. Fools, when quiet, are likely thinking of what they want to say. Hence, such a person isn't truly listening, at least not in a way to gain understanding.

The Active Listener

Communication is one of the most important life skills, and listening is a big part of that life skill. Unfortunately, much of the struggle with communication is directly related to a breakdown in listening. The challenge isn't a lack of hearing; instead, it is one of understanding. We hear but fail to grasp what is said. This is primarily due to a lack of focus and breakdowns in intellectual and emotional processes. Thus, the answer to many of the struggles in communication is active listening.

Active listening is about understanding. It is about going beyond merely hearing *what* is said and instead engaging *with* what is said. This may include paraphrasing back to the speaker what the speaker said, using body language to demonstrate the connection to what the speaker was saying, engaging in thoughtful questioning, and so on.

Such communication usually requires an investment of time and focus. It seldom occurs when one or more of the parties is in a hurry. It requires intentionality. Elements such as facial expressions, eye contact, displaying genuine interest in the speaker's words, offering attentive silence, and summarizing the speaker's points all revolve around the intentionality of communication.

Engaging in active listening requires a deliberate slowing down. It requires putting a brake on runaway thinking and resisting the urge to make a hurried response. It requires thinking about what is being said as well as the intent of what is being said. Active listening leads individuals to carefully reflect on their interaction with the message the speaker is trying to convey.

In contrast, *evaluative listeners* hear what the speaker is saying, but rather than fully engaging with it, they are more concerned with their response. They are thinking about what they want to say—the data they want to share, an alternate opinion, or an added-on statement or story. While they may be silent, it isn't attentive silence. They are simply waiting for the speaker to finish so they can respond. Even when attentive to evaluating every word, it is not with the intent of understanding what the speaker is communicating. It is to craft a response or a rebuttal. Hence, such listening is not active listening. It is evaluative listening. It is a lesser level of communication.

The Velocity of Thought

Our cognitive processes outpace spoken words; we think faster than we speak. While the average person utters 100–130 words per minute, research reveals that our brains can process a staggering eleven million bits of information per second unconsciously. The conscious mind, which can only handle forty to sixty bits per second, significantly outpaces the speech rate. This leads to challenges in effective listening, as our minds tend to wander, formulating responses and drawing conclusions that may not align with the speaker's intent (Pragya Agarwal, *Sway: Unravelling Unconscious Bias*).

Our ability to think faster than we speak leads to disengaged listeners. As hard as we might try not to tap into our spare thinking in order to listen well, we often fail. We might start well, listening to every word, intently focusing on what is being said, but before we know it, our subconscious brain (which has been working nonstop in the background) brings a thought to the forefront.

Consider the following. The speaker is one of your team members. You are trying your best to concentrate on what is being said, but your brain works at a much faster rate. Subconsciously, it brings to the forefront the thought *I need to be sure and tell them about* _________ *before the conversation is over*. The only common denominator is that it involves the speaker. It has nothing to do with what the speaker is saying.

The short trip to something else works. We quickly return to what the speaker is saying and haven't missed anything. Then we do it again. And again. At some point, we wander too far down a different road. When we return to what the speaker is saying, we discover we missed something of value. We are uncertain what it is, though. We are lost.

Unfortunately, this is much of what our communication consists of. We hear, but we don't listen. We receive, but we understand only a fraction of what was actually spoken. Perhaps the solution to listening well is what we do with our thinking while someone else is speaking.

Listening Can Be Taught

The good news is that although we struggle to listen, we can improve. As a next-level leader, this should be your desire. If you want to lead as well as possible, strive to become a better listener. Considering the statistic that only 5 percent receive training on how to listen, it is likely that you are a prime candidate. You can grow!

The ability to listen well isn't limited to being super smart or highly intelligent. To be a good listener, you must apply specific skills that can be acquired through teaching and training. Such training extends beyond the typical "Pay attention!" "Listen up!" and "Open your ears!" we have heard since childhood.

Tips for Active Listening

The following are simple steps anyone can take. There is nothing profound about them. But if you want to improve your listening ability, work on these things.

1. Resist the impulse to interrupt or interject. Allow the speaker to proceed without interruption. Concentrating on what the speaker is saying will help keep you from jumping to conclusions.
2. Listen beyond the spoken words. Effective communication encompasses more than verbal expression. Pay attention to nonverbal cues, such as body language and tone of voice. Seek to understand the speaker's emotions, ideas, and philosophies.
3. Master the art of paraphrasing. This is an excellent way to ensure you are understanding correctly. It is also a good way to help the speaker clarify the message. Say, "What I hear you saying is ______________." You may have to do this more than once while trying to confirm your understanding, but it is well worth the effort.
4. Stay focused. If your focus is wavering, bring it back to the present moment. When appropriate, this might entail you saying, "I'm sorry. Can you repeat that?" in your attempt to make sure you are focusing on what is being said.
5. Engage with notetaking. While it isn't always conducive to take notes, at times it can help.

Taking notes will help you stay focused on what the speaker is saying, create a track for what was said, enable you to recall it later, and communicate to the speaker that you are tuning in to what is being said.

6. Ask meaningful questions. Great listeners ask questions—but not just any questions. Some questions can come across as demeaning; thus, the intent of the question matters. Questions that help the speaker discover insight, clarify what the speaker is saying, or assist the listener in gaining additional understanding are of great value.
7. Embrace ideas over facts. Although facts are often of immense importance (for example, listening to directions), facts are typically shared to give shape to an idea. As an active listener, you don't want to get so focused on the facts that you miss out on the idea that the speaker is attempting to convey. Besides that, memorizing facts is often impossible; grasping the idea for which the facts were shared is much easier.

Team Conversations

My friend Mark is one of the 5 percent who have received training to become a better listener. His job sent him to Seattle, Washington, to go through high-level training on communication that has been taught to business leaders worldwide. I have had the privilege to listen to him share insights to effective communication, both in front of groups and in one-on-one conversations.

A portion of his training was on team conversations. I love teams, talking about teams, and working with teams. Teams, however, can be messy, and difficulties arise in getting everyone moving in the same direction. However, that should not discourage a leader from working with teams. Instead, it should challenge a leader to invoke best practices. As best-selling author Susan Scott maintains, one conversation at a time, we are either exceeding or failing. Thus, the team conversation is a significant factor in the team's ability to achieve success.

The practical tool Mark shared with me isn't the only conversation that teams have or should have. However, if you ever find the following occurring, then the principles my friend advocates are highly applicable.

- When you need to create an environment where different views can be safely shared.
- When you want to get everyone on the team moving in the same direction.
- When you as a leader are struggling to ascertain the best idea (not all best ideas come from you).
- To solicit multiple ideas (often competing ideas or perspectives).
- To develop a solid strategy.
- When the team is functioning in silos.

- When some team members control the conversation while others say little to nothing at all.
- When you ask a question and there is little to no response, or the response needs to be stronger in quality.

The chief principle behind the team conversation Mark shared with me is found within what is called the "beach ball model." Imagine a beach ball with multiple stripes of different colors. Everyone on the team represents a different color. You want to hear opposing ideas and gain insights that are different than you might have imagined. The only way to do this is for everyone to speak and do so with authenticity.

Here is one way to do this: Tell the team what you need from them. For example, "I have been mulling over __________ and have a couple ideas. We have tried ___________, and we've had some success with it but also some challenges. I would like to hear from you. What should we consider doing to improve things?"

Then start to your left and allow that person to share. Once the person is finished, simply say thank you. Do not say, "Wow, that is a great idea!" Why? There are two primary reasons: (1) it tells others on the team that their idea or thoughts aren't good, and (2) everyone will focus on one idea without listening to the others. Even when the team says, "Wow, that is a great idea," do not allow them to get sidetracked by focusing on that specific idea.

Instead, say, "Thank you. Let's listen to ________ ideas. I want to hear from everyone."

Often, some of the best ideas will be generated by the quieter team members. Just because they are quiet compared to others doesn't mean they don't have thoughts about the subject matter. Simply saying "thank you" and moving on to the next person, saying, "I would like to hear from ________. What do you think?" can go a long way in creating synergy.

Conclusion

When there is a perception that leaders aren't working well with others, many times this can be attributed to breakdowns in communication, which is often a breakdown in listening—not hearing something, hearing something but getting it distorted, or failing to understand what was being said. Such challenges, however, shouldn't cause a leader to take a dogmatic approach with others making communication one-directional: "I do the talking; you do the listening." This isn't to say that a leader cannot take the lead; it is simply to say that listening is more than hearing. Listening well is about participating in active listening.

When leaders engage in active listening, they build trust. Followers feel heard, supported, and safe. Such things cannot be achieved when the primary form of communication is one-directional, from the leader to the listener. One-directional communication is limiting; it limits the team from generating synergy. It is demoralizing and discouraging. While team members may perform, they will do so at a lesser level than they would have if they had only been heard.

As next-level leaders, we should strive to engage in active listening. Will we always get it right, hear everything we should hear, and understand everything the speaker attempts to convey? No. But that is not the point. The point is one of growth. It is about recognizing breakdowns in communication and seeking to do better.

CHAPTER 13

BE ATTENTIVE TO CULTURE

I was the new guy and wanted to make a good impression. Knowing that leadership is influence, I understood it would take time and effort to garner respect and build meaningful relationships. Therefore, I was as observant as possible in trying to fit in and meet the standard norms as I stepped into the role of a next-level leader.

Despite my best efforts, I overlooked it. Nobody briefed me on a certain rule. It wasn't covered in my job description or during the transition into my new role. While no one said a thing about it, no doubt several noticed when I failed to adhere to the expected norm.

Often, such violators of a standard norm are corrected. Those who have been there for some time think, *How could he have possibly missed it? Everyone knows you don't do* _________. Everyone, that is, except the new guy. It is challenging for those deeply ingrained in a culture to fathom how someone could be unaware. To them, the new guy is either incompetent or has willfully violated the expected norm.

So how did I eventually discover the unspoken rule? I observed. I noticed that my actions were different from the rest. While seemingly trivial in the grand scheme, it was, in fact, a rule, and I had unwittingly violated it. It took about five or six months before someone finally acknowledged the unspoken thing. I found it amusing that he referred to it as a rule one mustn't break—an anticipated behavior that had remained unarticulated until then. If I was going to succeed, I was going to have to learn the unspoken rules and adhere to them. Such is the nature of culture.

What Is Culture?

When people say they are trying to learn the ropes, they are essentially saying, "I'm trying to identify the expected norm." This is what I was trying to do. I had to figure out what was so familiar to everyone else that they naturally expected me to adhere to it, but unfortunately, it wasn't so familiar to me.

What is culture? It can be described as the proper way to behave within the organization. It is the silent code of conduct. It is the personality of a group or organization. Culture is the DNA of the organization. It is the overall vibe. It is about how people act and interact with one another.

Culture is powerful. It is the glue that keeps an organization together. Culture keeps things moving in a consistent manner and direction, resisting tugs and pulls from outliers. Hence, it consists of how people act and shapes how people behave (as it did in my case). It impacts what decisions are made and how they are made.

Culture can be defined as the shared values, attitudes, and practices that characterize an organization. It is complex and susceptible to change; however, it most often changes slowly. It is vulnerable; it depends on the values of the people who define it. Such people are key influencers, those who possess strong values that support existing values or bring health to an organization by tweaking or adding additional values.

Culture Eats Strategy for Breakfast

What does culture have to do with strategy? Peter Drucker, a widely known and influential thinker on management, famously said, "Culture eats strategy for breakfast." Someone else later added, "every day." In other words, an organization's shared values, attitudes, and practices are often much more important than the strategy.

Strategy defines direction and focus. It is needed and highly valuable. Where are we going? What should we do? Such questions pertain to strategy. Culture, however, largely determines whether the strategy will thrive or die by the wayside. While strategy focuses on resourcefulness and skillfulness, culture defines engagement, passion, and execution.

An organization's culture is a make-or-break factor in its ability to achieve vision and accomplish strategy. The real work isn't crafting a strategy; it is working the strategy, making it happen. No matter how detailed and solid a strategy is, the plan will fail if the culture isn't what it should be. The people within the organization must be passionate about the vision and enthusiastic about executing its plan. The strategy doesn't have a chance against the wrong culture.

An Example

I had been invited to look closely at the organization's inner workings. In doing so, I was fulfilling the role of a consultant. What I encountered was interesting. The core leadership team was deeply committed, albeit all relatively young and inexperienced. They possessed great attitudes and a desire to learn; they were engaging. But not all was well. Their strategy for growth stunk. It wasn't that it was terrible. In the right place, it would have been great. But not in this situation. It was contrary to the culture of the organization. The two—the culture and the strategy—were at odds with one another. I immediately recognized the outcome: culture was going to win. It always does. The strategy didn't have a chance.

Strategies often struggle to come to fruition due to the organization's culture. Unfortunately, most people fail to understand the breakdown. Some think the problem was the lack of vision-casting; others believe it was due to poor execution. All the while, it was neither. Instead, it was the fact that the strategy didn't fit the personality of the organization. An organization's strategy is subject to an organization's culture.

In this case, the strategy was designed to reach a specific segment of people. I didn't ask, but they assumed the strategy applied to all, not a particular group. Regardless, it didn't matter.

What intrigued me the most was their obliviousness to the inevitable failure of their strategy. Despite their well-crafted marketing plan and significant time investment, they seemed blind to the fact that it simply wouldn't work. They thought it was all about crafting a well-defined strategy, but it doesn't work that way. They should have looked closely at their culture.

Such is the power of culture. Strategy doesn't fail because of a lack of desire to accomplish a goal; strategy fails because of the personality of the organization.

Identifying Culture

Let's say you have assumed a leadership position as a next-level leader. This leadership position is in a new place, somewhere you haven't yet had ample time and exposure to learn the culture. You understand the importance of identifying cultural norms; you are trying to learn the ropes. How might you go about doing so?

Consider the following. Culture cannot be wrapped up in a sign or a job description. It isn't always that stark. Often it is subtle. It is right there before you, something you can see, feel, and hear, but not always in a loud or boisterous way.

For example, culture can be seen in how people talk. It may be formal or informal, open or selective, relaxed or intense. Culture can often be observed in the subject matter that drives a conversation. Consider the following: Is the culture more business-oriented or relationship-oriented? What is the primary subject matter? What do the leaders talk about? What is talked about speaks volumes.

Culture is not limited to what is said, however. Culture can be observed in the behavior of people. Are the people punctual? What does their body language say about things? What do they value (behavior reveals values)? Do they value excellence? Are they diligent in what they do? Do they understand the importance of a strong work ethic? Is the organization laid back? Or does the organization emphasize discipline and control?

Yet another way to identify the culture is to observe where the resources are allocated. Resources involve money, personnel, time, energy, and so on. Is there an investment in the growth and development of the people within the organization? Or is the focus primarily on expansion?

These are just a few of the many things you should look at when considering the culture. To thrive as a next-level leader, attentiveness to culture is essential.

Adjust to Existing Culture

As a next-level leader, it is essential that you adapt to culture. Hence, you must recognize the existing culture to succeed. That does not mean you must acquiesce to any unhealthy practices that might exist within a culture.

It simply means you cannot act contrary to the cultural norms. You have to adjust; you have to fit in.

Consider the following. You step into a leadership role within an existing culture exhibiting unhealthy practices. There is a measure of gossip that permeates the organization. Gatherings around the water cooler could be more positive. You don't have to join in and participate in gossip, but you do need to make sure you find a way to fit in.

Another example might be that raising one's voice in team meetings is common when one feels strongly about something. You don't have to raise your voice to be heard, but you can't be silent. You must join in.

Yet another example might be that side remarks are said in a way as to be funny, but you find little to laugh about. You don't have to make side remarks to fit in, but you might need to find a way to laugh and have fun in a meeting.

I have experienced such scenarios. While my values might have been contrary to the culture I was immersing myself in, I also understood one must use wisdom not to move too quickly in bucking the standard, especially if one has assumed a secondary leadership role within an organization. If you find yourself in a similar position, what should you do? Here are a few suggestions:

1. Respect cultural norms. Every culture has its own set of standards and values, including the one you are currently a part of. Pay attention to these norms and values and strive to respect

them. While you may make a few mistakes, minimizing them will help.

2. Build relationships. Connect with people in the culture you're adapting to and build relationships with them. If they know you care about them, want to know them, and are interested in them, they will go out of their way to assist and support you.
3. Ask questions. Be bold and ask questions about the culture, traditions, or expectations. Your desire to learn the culture will speak volumes to those within the organization. They will be more forgiving when you mess up, knowing that at least you have attempted to understand and adapt.
4. Assess and adjust your communication style. Wise leaders seek to adapt their communication style to fit the cultural context. This includes verbal and nonverbal communication. For example, some cultures prefer direct communication, while others prefer indirect. Some cultures may be assertive or aggressive, while others are more laid back. The point isn't that you must become something you are not. It is about developing the ability to adjust when needed.
5. Stay open-minded. Avoid making hasty decisions about what you do and don't like. Be open to new ideas, perspectives, and ways of doing things.

While you may see unhealthy aspects of the current culture, you can also identify positive things about the culture, things you would want to take with you should you move on elsewhere. Moreover, be cautious in wanting to impose a previous culture on a current one. In time, you may influence the culture, but it won't happen quickly.

6. Learn about the history. Seek to understand the historical background that has helped to shape the current culture; such understanding can be of immense value. There are reasons why certain things are valued; strive to understand why.
7. Dress appropriately. If you want to adapt to an existing culture, dress in a manner that aligns with the cultural norms. This is especially important in conservative or formal cultures. This might entail neckties, shoe styles, even the color of clothes.
8. Be patient. Adapting to a culture takes time. While some might expect immediate adaptation and be less forgiving of the mistakes you make, others will show great patience toward you. Regardless, strive to do your best to fit in. Be patient with others and with yourself as you navigate the process. You won't always get it right, but you can always have the right attitude while learning.

Remember that cultural adaptation is a two-way street, and it's not just about conforming but also about bringing your unique perspective and contributing positively to the culture you're entering. While you may not be able to control others, you can control yourself. Embrace the differences and similarities to the best of your ability while remaining true to your values.

Shaping Culture

Our job as leaders is to ensure the culture is healthy and conducive to the direction we want to go. Start by assessing the current culture. Is it healthy or toxic? What needs to change within the culture to get where you want to go? What impact does your personality and the personalities of the key influencers in the organization have on the current culture?

Leaders play a pivotal role in shaping organizational culture. Culture reflects the shared values, beliefs, behaviors, and norms within an organization, and it profoundly impacts how employees interact, make decisions, and perform their work. Here are some ways a leader can shape and influence the culture of an organization:

1. Set the example. Leaders set the tone for the organization's culture. Your team will closely observe your behavior, attitude, and work ethic.
2. Define the values. Clearly articulate the organization's core values and principles. Make sure these values align with the mission and

goals of the organization, and communicate them regularly,

3. Communicate the expectations. Define expectations for behavior and performance that align with the desired culture, and then make sure everyone clearly understands them.
4. Promptly address issues. When issues or conflicts arise, address them promptly and openly. Use these incidents as opportunities to reinforce the desired cultural norms.
5. Provide training. Offer training that reinforces cultural values and helps others to develop the necessary skills and mindset to thrive in the culture.
6. Give feedback. Regularly assess and evaluate the culture. Seek input from others to understand their experiences and perceptions. Use this information to make necessary adjustments and improvements.
7. Be consistent. Consistency is critical to maintaining and reinforcing the culture. Ensure that decisions, actions, and policies are aligned with the stated values.
8. Assess and adapt. Culture is not static; it evolves. Continuously monitor the culture, gather feedback, and be willing to adjust and refine it as the organization's needs and goals change.

Shaping and maintaining a healthy organizational culture is an ongoing process that requires commitment, dedication, and strong leadership. Leaders who prioritize culture will create an environment that is conducive to long-term success.

Preventing Cultural Drift

Cultural drift, sometimes called cultural erosion, occurs when the core values, beliefs, and behaviors that define an organization's culture gradually shift away from the desired or established cultural norms. This can happen over time due to various factors, such as changes in leadership or neglect of cultural maintenance. Cultural drift can be detrimental to an organization. It can lead to a misalignment between the stated culture and actual behaviors.

Preventing cultural drift requires a leader's active involvement and commitment. Here are steps a leader can take to avoid cultural drift within an organization (these steps are like those of shaping the culture).

1. Lead the way. As a leader, you are a role model for the organization's culture. Consistently embody the cultural values and behaviors you want to see in others. Your actions and words should align with the culture.
2. Talk about it. Regularly communicate the importance of the organization's culture. Talk about how the culture was formed from key

values and how alignment with those values will continue to shore up the desired culture. Use a variety of venues for communicating and reinforcing the desired culture.

3. Involve others. Encourage others at all levels of the organization to participate in helping to maintain the culture. Seek their input on cultural matters and involve them in discussions and initiatives relating to the culture.
4. Pay attention to whom you elevate. Pay careful attention to the people you bring on board as well as the onboarding process for those you elevate. Consider how they might fit in the culture. Are there areas of concern? If so, can you help them scale up early on so it doesn't cause difficulties later?
5. Train and develop. Provide training and development opportunities that help people maintain cultural standards and norms.
6. Continuously assess. Regularly assess the cultural health of an organization. Be open to adjusting as needed so the organization might remain healthy.
7. Maintain accountability to the culture. Hold team members accountable for adhering to cultural norms. Address any deviations from the culture promptly and constructively.
8. Incorporate cultural norms in decision-making. When making decisions, consider culture. Make

sure that decisions align with the values that drive the culture.

By actively engaging in the aforementioned practices, leaders can reduce the risk of cultural drift. In doing so, they will preserve a strong and thriving culture that aligns with the organization's purpose and values.

Conclusion

To be an effective leader, one must understand the underlying beliefs, values, and norms that guide his or her team or organization. Leaders must understand the organization's culture. Culturally aware leaders can better navigate challenges, conflicts, and opportunities and make decisions that align with the culture.

In summary, a next-level leader who is attentive to culture is better positioned to lead effectively, inspire the team, and drive positive organizational change. Understanding culture, or actively shaping a new one, is a fundamental aspect of leadership that can profoundly impact an organization's success.

CHAPTER 14

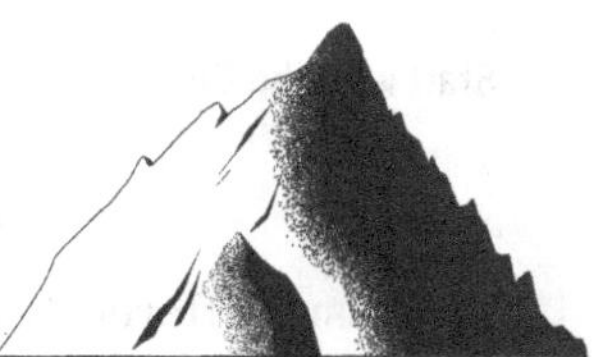

START WITH THE END IN MIND

Our family vacation is winding down, and this morning, like many others during these eleven days, I rose early. Why interrupt vacation bliss for sunrise and morning devotions? Picture this: It is a Colorado morning at 10,500 feet above sea level, and nature is putting on a breathtaking display outside our Airbnb's massive windows. The valley is adorned in green, the mountains painted in shades of blue, the sky with shades of orange. Words fall short of describing this spectacle. It is magnificent!

In this moment, my reflections turn to Revelation 13:8—Jesus, "the Lamb slain from the foundation of the world." God, the master planner, envisioned redemption long before Creation. Unlike us, He possesses omniscience—knowing all things at all times. While we lack this divine foresight, we can adopt a similar mindset, one where we start with the end in mind.

A Biblical Example

Jesus offered the best example of a next-level leader who starts with the end in mind. He stated in John 16:7, "Nevertheless I tell you the truth; it is expedient for you that I go away: for if I go not away, the Comforter will not come unto you; but if I depart, I will send him unto you." Jesus, looking into the future, understood that if the movement He was birthing were to succeed, it would require more than a single solitary leader. It would require an empowered team.

In contrast, Moses attempted to carry the burden of leadership alone. In doing so, he experienced symptoms of burnout. His "God let me die" prayer offers one example. He struggled to be a next-level leader due to an attempt to do leadership alone. Moses should have surveyed the scene and recognized early on that his way of leading wasn't sustainable. The load he was carrying was too heavy. He had assumed too many responsibilities. Moses should have sought other ways of meeting the needs of the people. He should have started with the end in mind.

Yet another example of Jesus starting with the end in mind is the Last Supper. Matthew detailed the preparations. The disciples were to find a specific man in the city, follow him to a house, and then speak to the owner of the house a particular message about using a room for a meal. During the Passover meal, Jesus instituted communion, using bread and wine to represent His body and blood that would soon be broken and poured out. Jesus knew what was about to happen and acted in ways that aligned with the future. And not only His immediate future but also the future of the church, as we, thousands of years later, still practice communion. Jesus acted with the end in mind.

A Personal Example

While in my early thirties, shortly after having been elected pastor, I began to consider the future. I was sure that one day we would experience growth, as the Lord had spoken it to me. However, I did not realize at the time that I would only be there for a season. The church would experience the growth we envisioned, but my role was planting and watering. Another man would experience the increase. At the time, however, I knew nothing of the sort. The Lord had directed me to go, and I had gone.

I envisioned us planting multiple churches, so we would need numerous pastors. My primary responsibility would be to equip the leaders. Others would pastor the congregations. I would relinquish control for something better—empowering others. With this resolve, I started looking for a possible successor; I did this when we were just getting started. I didn't know what to call it, but I was starting with the end in mind.

A few years later, God moved us elsewhere. The young man I believed would pastor the church moved on as well. Perhaps you are thinking, *One of them, if not both, missed it.* If so, you need more information.

While things did not unfold as I had envisioned, much of what I dreamed about happened, but on a much larger scale than I ever thought possible. I have written multiple leadership books that have been published in numerous languages, traveled at home and abroad teaching and training leaders, and, as of this writing, am presently serving as the president of a Bible college where we train future leaders. I am nothing special. It has been a God thing. God placed the desires in my heart. He called me; I didn't call myself. God opened the doors, and I walked through them. My primary responsibility has been to steward what God has placed in my hands through the years. My studies and personal growth were necessary, but I didn't make my future happen. It was God who made it happen. I was simply stewarding what was in my hands.

Moreover, the young man whom I thought would become the next pastor moved on to assist a friend of mine. They have made a wonderful team for over two decades. I couldn't be prouder of him and his wife. We did what we knew to do at the time; God prepared us for something more, then placed us in position to see it come to fruition.

Notice that starting with the end in mind is not an exact science; it is a progression. It is a journey that has many turns and curves. I am a strong advocate, however, that despite the unknowns, it doesn't mean you shouldn't start with the end in mind. Although it won't turn out exactly as you envision it, envision things anyway. If you don't have the end in mind, you will never get started, or you will become sidetracked with other things. You will become discouraged and lose sight of where you are headed. In short, starting with the end in mind allows you to plan accordingly while being flexible.

A Successional Mindset

As I have assumed various roles and responsibilities of leadership, I have sought to look ahead and plan accordingly. Knowing that all leadership is temporary, I understand that in time someone else will take the lead. I will move on to something else and another will step into the leadership role. I still must engage with the process even though choosing my successor is outside my control. Yet knowing I will move off the scene one day, I often think, *This person might be the next leader*.

Furthermore, because I care about the organization I am leading (if you don't care, don't ever assume the leadership role), I want the organization to succeed, especially after I am gone. What kind of a leader would I be if I thought otherwise? Certainly not the type of leader I want to be. Knowing this, I want to pour into others, equipping them for when they will step into another leadership level. Starting with the end in mind allows me to participate in this endeavor—helping others become next-level leaders regardless of whether one of them is my successor. Equipping others is simply the right thing to do at all times.

While engaging in the thought process of pondering who might be my successor, I am constantly reminded that the leadership position I am serving in is simply that: a leadership position. It is a role I fulfill. It is not *who* I am. Neither does it validate me. My validation comes from God, not a title.

Thinking about succession also reminds me that the position is not mine. It is a role I serve in for a period of time. My responsibility is to be faithful to what God has entrusted to me, to be a good steward of what He has placed in my hand. In time, it will be the responsibility of another. And after that person, then another. Those leaders will be judged (as I will be), with what they do with what has been entrusted to them. I hope they will outshine anything I have ever done. To think otherwise would be arrogant. Why wouldn't I or any other leader want things to be better? After all, the goal isn't for a leader to look good; the goal is for the common purpose to be accomplished.

More Than Succession

There is more to starting with the end in mind than succession, however. It also includes identifying what needs to be accomplished.

Think about it. Jesus used the analogy of building a tower to illustrate the importance of counting the cost before beginning a task:

> For which of you, desiring to build a tower, does not first sit down and count the cost, whether he has enough to complete it? Otherwise, when he has laid a foundation and cannot finish, all who see it begin to mock him, saying, "This

man began to build and was not able to finish."
(Luke 14:28–30, ESV)

While this passage of Scripture does not use the exact phrase "start with the end in mind," it does convey the importance of planning and considering the outcomes of one's actions. The way to get to where you are headed is first to know where you want to go. It is so simple that it can easily be overlooked. Starting with the end in mind is much deeper, richer, and more valuable than most people understand.

Stephen Covey likely influenced the writing of this chapter. After making multiple notes and writing significant portions of the chapter, I recalled encountering something similar to what I was addressing. Sure enough, it didn't take long to find it. It is in Covey's book *The 7 Habits of Highly Effective People*. According to Covey, highly effective people "begin with the end in mind." In other words, highly effective people can envision what they cannot see with their eyes. It is based on the principle that all things are created twice—once in the mind; second, in reality.

Consider the value of applying *starting with the end in mind* to the following:

- Each day: Where do you want to be at the end of the day? What do you want to have accomplished?
- Tasks: What is the desired end? What will it look like if you accomplish what you set out to

do? Knowing this up-front will help you stay on target.
- Projects: What is the desired outcome of the project? Knowing the desired end will help you navigate the journey as other things will arise that will distract you.
- Your Life: What do you want to accomplish by the end of your life? Have you thought about it? Have you distilled it into a personal mission statement?

These are just a few ways next-level leaders can start with the end in mind.

Stair-Step What?

A few months after I had moved across the state to assume a full-time pastoral role, I met with the senior pastor. He asked me what my vision was for family ministries. I replied, "Whatever your vision is." He smiled and said, "I appreciate that, but I want to know your vision." I said, "Seriously, you are the senior pastor. Tell me what you want accomplished, and I will do my best to make it happen." To my surprise, he smiled ever-so-slightly and said, "I can tell this isn't going anywhere, so here it is. My vision is for Eugene and Kerri Wilson to come here and launch the family ministries. Now, what is your vision for the ministry?" It was a liberating moment for me, as I am a big-picture, visionary person.

Given the green light, I excitedly shared my vision for family ministries with him. What he said in response left me wondering what was about to happen. He said, "That's all wonderful. Sounds exciting. You need to stair-step all of that." My look must have said a lot because he quickly asked, "You don't know what I mean, do you?" I replied, "No, sir." He said, "Don't worry about it. Get with my daughter, Chrystal. She knows how to stair-step things. She will show you how."

A few days later, Chrystal and I met. I said, "Your dad wants me to stair-step my vision. What is he talking about?" Although that was some years ago, I'm pretty sure she chuckled. She said, "I see you want to have a marriage retreat in August (it was October at the time). I assume you want to do a banquet on Friday night, correct?" I said yes. She then asked, "How many bowls do you need?" I said, "What?" She remarked, "If you want to have a banquet, I assume you want to serve salads. How many bowls do you need?" With a look of puzzlement (I'm sure I gave her a look too), I remarked, "I don't have a clue."

She said, "The number of bowls is based on the estimated number of people attending the banquet." She added, "Do you think the number might be around 120–130 people?" I said yes. She said, "Okay," and began writing the number down on a piece of paper. She lifted the paper to show me what she was doing while explaining, "This is a form the lady who oversees the kitchen will receive. She receives forms like this from other ministries too. She then orders what is needed in bulk. It helps cut expenses and frees you, and others like you, from worrying about such supplies when the time arrives." She added, "This is what stair-stepping looks like. We have multiple forms to fill out, such as audio-video, announcements, and the like for each event."

Approximately fifteen minutes later, she looked at me and asked, "Do you have a headache?" (I was holding my head in my hands.) To which I replied, "Yes." It wasn't until a similar meeting a few weeks later when I got another headache that I figured it out. My head was hurting because I was using parts of my brain I had never used before.

Although that was years ago, I think of it often. Chrystal impacted my life greatly as she taught me how to stair-step things. I would go on to apply those lessons in many other areas of my life. Don't miss this—you can only stair-step what you first envision. You have to start with the end in mind.

Strategic Planning

Stair-stepping is a strategic approach to planning that transforms visionary goals into manageable, actionable steps. It involves breaking down a grand vision into incremental stages, each building upon the last, like an ascending staircase toward a lofty objective.

It's a methodology that ensures each step is purposeful, each stage well-supported, and each accomplishment a building block toward the realization of your overarching vision. In essence, stair-stepping is the blueprint for turning dreams into reality, one step at a time.

Nehemiah's Example

Consider the following biblical example. Nehemiah was a high-ranking official in the court of King Artaxerxes I of Persia. Having received news concerning the dire condition of Jerusalem's wall, Nehemiah felt a strong sense of responsibility to address the issue. Permitted to act, he made his way to Jerusalem, where he first assessed the situation by inspecting the walls and gates. He then developed a detailed plan of action and began working on it. First, he met with the people to communicate the plan to them. Then he gathered the materials needed to accomplish the job, organized the people, and delegated responsibilities. Despite tremendous obstacles, Nehemiah and the people completed the rebuilding of the walls in only fifty-two days, a fantastic accomplishment. Notice that he started with the end in mind.

Similarly, we can follow Nehemiah's methodology. First, assess the situation. Second, develop a plan. Third, communicate the plan. And fourth, overcome challenges. Such is the importance and value of a strategic plan. It helps bring alignment to the team and points the way forward. When everyone on the team moves in the same direction, great things can be accomplished. And getting everyone on the team moving in the same direction involves starting with the end in mind.

Unfortunately, most people consider strategy an annual event. But that's not how things work in real life. Things change. There are unanticipated threats as well as opportunities. Ultimately, the strategy that leads to success isn't a static one; it is the one that evolves while remaining true to the desired end result.

Do This When Engaging in Strategic Planning

Here are a few more details to consider when engaging in strategic planning as a next-level leader.

1. Define the end goal. Clearly articulate the desired result while making sure the goal is realistic and aligned with the overall vision.
2. Envision success. Develop a word picture of what success looks like and then use the image as motivation throughout the planning and execution phases.
3. Develop a plan of action. As mentioned before, outline the steps and strategies required to achieve the end goal. Be sure to include potential challenges.
4. Prioritize the plan. Focus on the most critical elements first, then continue to assess the MIT (most important thing) needed to move things forward.
5. Stair-step the plan. Divide overarching goals into smaller, achievable tasks, thereby making progress measurable and executable.
6. Anticipate challenges. Identify potential obstacles and challenges. Do your best not to get caught by surprise when challenges arise.

7. Be flexible. Recognize that things may change. Be open to adapting the plan if needed.
8. Review and reflect. Regularly assess progress of the plan. Ask, "What's working well?" and "What needs to be adjusted?" Then make the necessary changes.

There will be many challenges along the way, filled with plenty of opportunities to quit. Starting with the end in mind will best position you to succeed as a next-level leader.

Conclusion

I started this chapter in July while on vacation in Colorado. It is now November. No, it hasn't taken me that long to write this chapter—I shifted my writing to other chapters. At this moment, I am looking at the Atlantic Ocean from the balcony of an Airbnb on Hilton Head Island, South Carolina. I am not on vacation, although I did watch the sunrise just a few minutes ago. I am here for a minister's retreat called *Sozo*. (*Sozo* is a Greek word meaning "to make whole" or "be whole." It is used often in Scripture.)

We started the journey with the Sozo team three years ago with online brainstorming meetings and face-to-face planning meetings. It has taken an enormous amount of time and required an investment of energy and resources. The cause, however, compelled us forward. Our involvement stems mainly from a vision birthed out of a burden my wife carries. Kerri has wanted to host a minister's retreat for some years. It is a big part of why she returned to school to obtain a doctorate in pastoral care and counseling. She is not the only one with the burden; others with a similar passion have joined this endeavor.

We started this week with the end in mind. We started this endeavor to make a difference in the lives of ministers. It will likely take years before what we envision comes to fruition; things of this magnitude always do. The way forward, however, is by first starting with the end in mind.

I have written most of this book—thirty minutes here and there, often early in the morning. It has taken some time, but starting with the end in mind has enabled me to get here. I am almost done and anxiously await getting started on another book. I will start that one with the end in mind too.

CHAPTER 15

AIM TO FINISH WELL

I was around nine years old, sitting in the back seat of a car, listening to a furniture store manager share his story. Earlier in life, he had been a pastor and preached at youth camps my father and uncle had attended. But he was no longer active in the ministry; he sold furniture. I will never forget the impression he made as he said, "The crazy thing is when I fell, I was praying more than ever." Later, on our way back to my uncle's house, the discussion in the car centered on how one could fall away while praying. The conclusion was that one could go through the motions of praying but never genuinely pray.

It is still difficult for me to wrap my head around it all. Unfortunately, I have witnessed similar stories of men whom God used mightily, who later became a shell of what they once were. I am sure leaders fall for a variety of reasons. A quick survey of Scripture reveals some. Regardless of all the reasons, all have one thing in common—they failed to finish well.

Struggling to Finish Well

Some do not fall as far as others, yet still fail to finish as well as they started. Consider David, a man after God's heart, who committed adultery. Or Moses, a phenomenal servant leader who allowed the frustrations of ministry to drive him to act in ways unpleasing to God. Finishing well isn't just about not getting derailed. Finishing well also encompasses overcoming such things as complacency, bitterness, and callousness while staying true to one's principles amid challenges.

Notice the following who were positioned to make a substantial difference in the world, but who, for various reasons, failed to finish well. We can learn from their stories.

Solomon

Solomon started well. "Solomon the son of David established himself in his kingdom, and the LORD his God was with him and made him exceedingly great" (II Chronicles 1:1, ESV). According to II Chronicles 1, Solomon demonstrated his reverence for and reliance upon God by sacrificing a thousand bulls on the altar in Gibeon. That night God appeared to Solomon in a dream and said, "Ask what I shall give you" (II Chronicles 1:7, ESV). Solomon's response was to ask for wisdom to lead God's people well, which God rewarded with riches as well as wisdom (II Chronicles 1:11–12).

Solomon had it made. He had the smoothest start of any king in Israel's history. He inherited a well-stocked stable, a firmly established kingdom, and an abundance of available resources. He was well equipped to construct the first temple in Jerusalem, also known as Solomon's Temple. But that's not all he built. He also constructed an elaborate palace complex for himself, which included the House of the Forest of Lebanon and a palace for the daughter of Pharaoh, whom he married. Furthermore, he fortified and built up various cities in Israel, including repairing and completing the wall of Jerusalem.

Despite Solomon's accomplishments and advantages, he could have finished better.

> [Solomon] had 700 wives, who were princesses, and 300 concubines. And his wives turned away his heart. For when Solomon was old his wives turned away his heart after other gods, and his heart was not wholly true to the Lord his God, as was the heart of David his father. (I Kings 11:3–4, ESV)

Although he had great wealth and fame, Solomon became a cynical old man. He is an example of a great leader who failed to finish well.

Jeroboam

Here's a synopsis of Jeroboam, a servant of Solomon. Jeroboam was an industrious young man and a brave warrior. After Solomon's death, the northern tribes approached King Rehoboam, Solomon's son, asking for a reduction in the heavy labor and taxes that Solomon had imposed on them. When Rehoboam refused to lighten their burden, the ten northern tribes rebelled, and Jeroboam was chosen as their leader.

God gave Jeroboam rules for a successful reign. He would succeed in leading a nation through his relationship with God and God alone.

> If you will listen to all that I command you, and will walk in my ways, and do what is right in my eyes by keeping my statutes and my commandments, as David my servant did, I will be with you and will build you a sure house, as I built for David, and I will give Israel to you. (I Kings 11:38, ESV)

Rather than heed the word of the Lord, Jeroboam chose to heed the voice of his counsel. God, however, did not give up on him. Instead, He made repeated attempts to renew His relationship with Jeroboam. Yet Jeroboam stubbornly refused.

A close look at Jeroboam's life through I Kings reveals he had all the traits to be an extraordinary leader. He was proactive, organized, visionary, ambitious, and possessed personal charisma. His ability to influence others was tremendous. But more is needed than great charisma.

One can have immense charm and the ability to control many, be organized, and efficiently lead others, and still not finish well. To finish well, one must utilize one's ability to lead others in a way that is pleasing to God. God wanted a nation that loved and obeyed Him. Jeroboam failed to lead in a way that led others toward God. Despite his tremendous leadership abilities, he stands out as one of the worst leaders in biblical history.

Rehoboam

While Jeroboam ruled the ten northern tribes, Rehoboam was king of Judah, including Benjamin. Upon the death of his father, Solomon, Rehoboam inherited the throne when he was forty-one years old.

A study of the life of Rehoboam offers some interesting insights. The Bible says Rehoboam reigned for seventeen years but served the Lord for only three of those years. His story came to a tragic end, as noted in II Chronicles 12:14 (NKJV), "And he did evil, because he did not prepare his heart to seek the Lord."

In contrast, Rehoboam's grandfather, King David, was a man after God's heart. What is the telling difference between the two men? While David fixed his heart (Psalm 57:7), Rehoboam did not. There were times in which Rehoboam turned toward God, times in which he desired God, and times in which he worshiped God. But Rehoboam never prepared or fixed his heart to seek the Lord. Therefore, the Bible declares he did evil. Despite his pedigree, Rehoboam failed to realize that how one finishes is as essential, if not more so, than one's early successes.

Finishing Well

Paul understood that much can be learned by studying the lives of other leaders. He wrote in Romans 15:4 (NIV), "For everything that was written in the past was written to teach us, so that through the endurance taught in the Scriptures and the encouragement they provide we might have hope." In I Corinthians 10:6 (NIV), while referring to the stories of God's people in the Old Testament, Paul wrote, "Now these things occurred as examples to keep us from setting our hearts on evil things as they did." Wise leaders will learn from the mistakes of others and train themselves to avoid them.

So what do leaders who finish well excel at doing? One study found that leaders who end well demonstrate several of the following characteristics, and some demonstrate as many as four or five.

1. They maintain a vibrant relationship with God.
2. They maintain a learning posture.
3. They manifest a Christlike character.
4. They live the truth.
5. They leave behind one or more substantial contributions.
6. They possess an ever-growing awareness of destiny.

Daniel

When considering biblical characters who finished well, one should look at the life of Daniel. Notice the following:

1. His faith. Throughout his life, Daniel faced numerous challenges that tested his faith, yet he remained steadfast in his faithfulness. This was seen in his life and the lives of his friends when they refused to eat the king's food, and in his continuing to pray despite a decree against it.
2. His dependency on God. Daniel's interpretation of dreams showcased his dependency on God. This dependency ensured that he could navigate complex situations and maintain his integrity while doing so.
3. His courage. Daniel's actions that resulted in his being thrown into the lions' den are a testament to Daniel's courage. Even though he was threatened with death, he continued to pray and trust in God. This courage extended beyond that moment, however, as Daniel displayed a willingness to confront kings with difficult truths.
4. His integrity. Daniel's integrity was unwavering. This is seen in that while he was involved in service to Babylonian and Persian rulers, he remained honest, humble, and ultimately, loyal to God.

The Apostle Paul

While Daniel is an Old Testament example of someone who finished well, Paul is a New Testament example of the same. Notice the words of the apostle Paul, who, while nearing the end of his life and ministry, penned the following: "I have fought the good fight, I have finished the race, I have kept the faith" (II Timothy 4:7, NIV).

Paul's use of the images of a soldier and an athlete, both of which require great discipline, offers insight into how he finished well. In I Corinthians, Paul appears to make a direct correlation between training for spiritual things with training for the local version of the Olympic Games.

> Do you not know that in a race all the runners run, but only one gets the prize? Run in such a way as to get the prize. Everyone who competes in the games goes into strict training. They do it to get a crown that will not last, but we do it to get a crown that will last forever. (I Corinthians 9:24–25, NIV)

To state that Paul had participated in training and was thus well-equipped would be an understatement. He continued,

> I therefore so run, not as uncertainly; so fight I, not as one that beateth the air: but I keep under my body, and bring it into subjection:

> lest that by any means, when I have preached to others, I myself should be a castaway. (I Corinthians 9:26–27)

Considering that Paul had been shipwrecked three times, beaten multiple times, and lived in constant danger yet did not back down, one can easily derive he was well-disciplined. Even as Paul penned the words "I have fought the good fight, I have finished the race, I have kept the faith," he was in prison and would soon be martyred. His participation in training, however, had equipped him to finish well. His end was not filled with gloom and despair. It wasn't even seen in his writings. Instead, at the end he was offering words of exhortation: "Run on. Fight on. Don't quit. Aim to finish strong."

The apostle Paul was probably around sixty years old when he penned the following to Pastor Timothy: "Train yourself to be godly. For physical training is of some value, but godliness has value for all things, holding promise for both the present life and the life to come" (I Timothy 4:7–8, NIV). Lifelong spiritual training made it possible for Paul to finish strongly.

Barriers to Finishing Well

Dr. J. Robert Clinton, whose research was addressed in chapter 4, identified six barriers that hinder leaders from finishing well: (1) the misuse of money, (2) the abuse of power, (3) pride, (4) sexual misconduct, (5) family dissension, and (6) complacency. While any one of the barriers can result in a leader failing to finish well, what is most interesting is that each barrier is deeply rooted in character issues rather than leadership skills. Thus, finishing well isn't about leadership ability as much as formability; it is contingent on the leader's commitment to being shaped into Christ's likeness.

What is formability? Formability, in the context of leadership, refers to a leader's openness and willingness to be molded or shaped, particularly to come into alignment with biblical principles of character and biblical values. It emphasizes the leader's receptiveness to personal growth, ethical development, and alignment with God's plan and purpose for the leader's life. Leaders with high formability recognize the ongoing need to be shaped into a more Christlike character, to give themselves to more than the development of mere leadership skills.

A leader's character issues ultimately influence decision-making, interactions, and overall conduct. In the context of leadership, character issues are foundational to the leader's identity, influencing how a leader navigates challenges, treats others, and upholds ethical standards. It is easy to see, one's level of formability can greatly impact one's trajectory.

Leadership skills, which involve the practical abilities, competencies, and techniques that contribute to effective leadership, are needed. This includes strategic thinking, communication prowess, decision-making acumen, and the capacity to inspire and guide a team. However, while leadership skills are undoubtedly crucial, they operate on the foundation of character.

A key distinction between the two—leadership skill set and a leader's character or Christlikeness—lies in the source and sustainability of both. Leadership skills can be learned and refined over time, but character issues are deeply rooted in one's moral fabric. The danger arises when leadership skills outpace the development of character. A leader might excel in skills, but without a solid character foundation, may succumb to pitfalls like misuse of power, pride, or complacency.

As one moves toward the finish line, the emphasis on formability increases. Enduring success hinges more on character development than on the mastery of leadership skills. Thus, formability, the willingness to be shaped into Christlike character, becomes the cornerstone of finishing well.

Ending Musings

As I write the closing portion of this book, the theme of finishing well resonates deeply within me. Reflecting on the past twenty or so years, little has changed in so many ways. From typing school papers in airplanes to writing discussion posts while my wife drove, the pursuit of knowledge and leadership development has been a constant companion. It is still a major component of my life. The goal has always been clear—to run well, to end well.

As a student, I never asked for assignment extensions. For me, I viewed it as part of my development. It was as vital, if not more so, than the knowledge acquired from the assignments themselves. I wanted to grow, to become a better me. I wanted to execute my responsibilities to the best of my ability.

As I write, we are cruising high above the earth headed toward Taiwan. The hum of the aircraft and the absence of distractions have helped to create a moment for reflection. I have observed the hustle and aimless busyness of those caught in the cycle of a spinning wheel. I've come to understand that mere activity doesn't equate to meaningful progress, and that true essence lies not in constant motion but in purposeful movement—actions that align with a higher calling.

Unfortunately, I've witnessed some who were aligned with their purpose, but who, for whatever reason, faltered in the final stretch. Some succumbed to moral failures. Others settled for comfort over sacrifice, choosing a false sense of validation that was based on accomplishments and possessions rather than His call.

This brings me back to the heart of leadership—pursuing a life of becoming all God wants us to be, with a strong commitment to finishing well. It's not just about attaining success in the present but ensuring that the journey concludes with integrity and purpose. We must understand that what we are currently constructing and working toward is precisely what we will leave behind.

For now, my journey, like yours, continues. The lessons we learned from Daniel, Paul, and other biblical characters serve as guiding stars. They propel us forward, urging us to maintain a vibrant relationship with our calling, to embody the attributes of those who finished well, and to stay attuned to the ever-growing awareness of our destiny. May we do as they did; may we, too, finish well.